A NEW DAWN:

Society and Politics
in the Light of Initiatic Science

New translation from the French
Original title: LE VERSEAU ET L'AVÈNEMENT
DE L'AGE D'OR

Prosveta S.A. – B.P. 12 – 83601 Fréjus Cedex (France)

ISBN 2-85566-486-1
édition originale: ISBN 2-85566-242-7

Omraam Mikhaël Aïvanhov

A NEW DAWN:
Society and Politics
in the Light of Initiatic Science
Part 1

2nd edition

Complete Works — Volume 25

EDITIONS PROSVETA

Editor-Distributor

Editions PROSVETA S.A. – B.P. 12 – 83601 Fréjus Cedex (France)

Distributors

AUSTRIA
MANDALA
Verlagsauslieferung für Esoterik
A-6094 Axams, Innsbruckstraße 7

BELGIUM
PROSVETA BENELUX
Van Putlei 105 B-2548 Lint
N.V. MAKLU Somersstraat 13-15
B-2000 Antwerpen
VANDER S.A.
Av. des Volontaires 321
B-1150 Bruxelles

BRAZIL
NOBEL SA
Rua da Balsa, 559
CEP 02910 - São Paulo, SP

BRITISH ISLES
PROSVETA Ltd
The Doves Nest
Duddleswell, Uckfield,
East Sussex TN22 3JJ
Trade orders to :
ELEMENT Books Ltd
Unit 25, Longmead, Shaftesbury
Dorset SP7 8PL

CANADA
PROSVETA Inc.
1565 Montée Masson
Duvernay est, Laval, Que. H7E 4P2

GERMANY
EDIS GmbH
Daimlerstr.5
D - 8029 Sauerlach

GREECE
PROFIM MARKETING Ltd
Ifitou 13
17563 P. Faliro
Athens

HOLLAND
STICHTING
PROSVETA NEDERLAND
Zeestraat 50
2042 LC Zandvoort

HONG KONG
HELIOS – J. Ryan
P.O. BOX 8503
General Post Office, Hong Kong

IRELAND
PROSVETA IRL.
84 Irishtown – Clonmel

ITALY
PROSVETA Coop. a r.l.
Cas. post. 13046 – 20130 Milano

LUXEMBOURG
PROSVETA BENELUX
Van Putlei 105 B-2548 Lint

NORWAY
PROSVETA NORDEN
Postboks 5101
1501 Moss

PORTUGAL
PUBLICAÇÕES
EUROPA-AMERICA Ltd
Est Lisboa-Sintra KM 14
2726 Mem Martins Codex

SPAIN
ASOCIACIÓN PROSVETA ESPAÑOLA
C/ Ausias March n° 23 Ático
SP-08010 Barcelona

SWITZERLAND
PROSVETA
Société Coopérative
CH - 1808 Les Monts-de-Corsier

UNITED STATES
PROSVETA U.S.A.
P.O. Box 49614
Los Angeles, California 90049

VENEZUELA
J.P. Leroy
Apartado 51 745
Sabana Grande
1050 A – Caracas

Readers will better understand certain aspects of the lectures published in the present volume if they bear in mind that the Master Omraam Mikhaël Aïvanhov's Teaching was exclusively oral and that the editors have made every effort to respect the flavour and style of each lecture.

The Master's Teaching is more than a body of doctrines: it is an organic whole, and his way of presenting it was to approach it from countless different points of view. By repeating certain aspects in a wide variety of contexts he constantly reveals a new dimension of the Whole and, at the same time, throws new light on the individual aspects and on their vital links with each other.

Omraam Mikhaël Aïvanhov

TABLE OF CONTENTS

Chapter One

The Age of Aquarius

In the Apocalypse, St John describes the four Holy Living Creatures who stand before the Throne of God singing, day and night: 'Holy, holy, holy, Lord God Almighty, Who was and is and is to come!' The first living creature was like a lion, the second like a calf, the third resembled a man and the fourth was like an eagle. These are the same four animals that we find in the two axes of the Zodiac formed by the polar opposites Leo-Aquarius and Taurus-Scorpio. You will object that there is no eagle in the Zodiac, that the sign opposite Taurus is Scorpio. That is true but, in the past, the Eagle occupied the place that is now given to Scorpio; it was when man committed original sin by his failure to master his sexual energy that the eagle fell (symbolically) from its place in the heavens and became a scorpion, Scorpio. And, incidentally, the correspondences defined by the Initiates between the different parts of the human body and the signs of the Zodiac indicate that Scorpio corresponds to the genitals.

Aquarius, which is an air sign, represents man and, hence, thought and knowledge. The age of Aquarius will be the age of knowledge... but not the intellectual knowledge that turns human beings into dried up mummies. Nowadays, people are very learned and well informed but they are not alive. Aquarius is represented as an old man pouring water from an urn: the old man is wisdom and the water flowing from his urn is the water of life. The knowledge brought by Aquarius is a knowledge that arouses, awakens and bestows life. Human beings may know everything there is to know about microbes or the stars but one cannot help but be horrified to see how they behave in their everyday lives. They possess everything except the one thing that is essential: the knowledge of how to live.

The water pouring from the old man's urn teaches human beings that everything in and around them must be cared for, nourished and watered and brought to fruition. The emblem of the Brotherhood, the anchor with the stream of water flowing from two hands, is also a symbol of Aquarius. And in Greek mythology Aquarius is represented by Ganymede, the 'cupbearer of the gods'.

Water is life-giving but, as human beings have forgotten about water, they are not irrigated — or, if they are, what with? What they need above all else is the water of life, living water. This is why, although Aquarius is a symbol of knowledge, it is not the knowledge of the brain but of the solar plexus, for only the solar plexus can cause the living water to flow in the bosom of man. We read in the Gospels, 'Out of his heart will flow rivers of living water.' The coming of Aquarius was already foretold in these words, but in a form which no one could understand at the time.

However learned your words may be, if they do not contain the living water they will always be theoretical and lifeless. This is the trouble with our culture today: human beings possess a mass of information but it is all superficial; it is not alive. For my part, I would rather possess the science of life than all the knowledge found in books for, once I know how to live, that is to say, once I know how to vibrate in unison and in harmony with the laws of the cosmos, the universe itself will be an open book to me. This is why the Teaching of the Universal White Brotherhood brings an entirely new element into the world. Human beings display their immense science and I am deeply impressed, it is truly extraordinary, but it is not vital. The only thing that is of vital importance is to live in harmony with the laws of the cosmos.

I have often told you that there are two kinds of knowledge. That which is dispensed in universities and which brings with it social status, money and prestige but which is incapable of transforming you. It leaves you exactly as it found you: if you were sensual you will continue to be sensual; if you were miserly you will continue to be a miser, etc. Then there is the other kind of knowledge, that of the Initiates, and it bestows neither prestige nor wealth but it will not leave you as it found you. And this is the knowledge that Aquarius brings, the knowledge that transforms and vivifies.

Astrologers and esoterics have been talking about the coming of the Age of Aquarius for years although, in reality, the vernal point will actually enter the constellation of Aquarius only in two hundred years from now. However it is only to be expected that its influence should already make itself felt. In the month of March it is still winter but there are days when the sun, the birds and the flowers tell us that spring is in the air. Before the season is actually there, we sense its presence; it is already with us thanks to its emanations, its fragrance, its aura. In the same way, all the modern discoveries in the field of atomic physics and space are signs of the approaching 'season' of Aquarius.

Aquarius is an air sign. This is why, ever since the influences of this sign began to make themselves felt, scientific research has focussed to a large degree on the things of air: flight and the use of air in general. During the Piscean age, scientific discoveries were principally in the area of water and navigation. Today, with Aquarius, we are entering the domain of air: telecommunications (telephone, television, etc.), planes, rockets and so on. And if there are still a great many accidents in the air, it is because men fail to understand that the atmosphere is like the ocean, that it has the same currents, waves and disturbances as water.

Although we have not fully entered the Age of Aquarius yet,

we are already experiencing some tremendous upheavals. This is because Aquarius is under the rulership of Saturn and Uranus. In fact, it is this influence that is a little alarming, for Saturn has a tendency to restrict, obstruct and destroy whereas Uranus tends to provoke accidents and explosions: all forms of explosion are due to the influence of Uranus. Aquarius, therefore, necessarily involves a certain amount of breakage: it is going to have to break through existing structures in order to propagate its ideas of universality.

Aquarius, as we have said, is shown as an old man pouring water from an urn. His water is the living water of the new Teaching, and people whose birth charts show several planets in Aquarius are particularly well prepared to pick up the new waves coming from this constellation. It is they who become innovators and inventors. The many discoveries that are being made today in the psychic and esoteric fields are triggered by Aquarius; also, anything that has to do with the notion of collectivity and universal brotherhood. In fact, before long, everybody is going to have to grow in awareness and understanding of the notion of brotherhood and universality. And, for you, universality will mean that, instead of being attached to only a few people, a husband or wife and children, your ideal is to be immersed, with all other human beings, in the cosmic ocean of life, love, beauty and joy.

The Piscean Age was the age of Christianity and it was characterized by exactly those qualities that correspond to Pisces, the sign of self-abnegation and sacrifice. Before that came the Arien Age in which the religion of Moses flourished and, before that again, the Taurean Age, with the Egyptian and Babylonian religions. The Age of Aquarius will bring new life. In the beginning, we shall witness some gigantic upheavals in the world but these will give birth to a Golden Age. The new Golden Age will be the fruit of the Age of Aquarius.

Vidélinata (Switzerland), December 10, 1966

Chapter Two

The Dawn of Universal Brotherhood

I

Human beings imagine that they have been put on this earth to eat and drink, have a good time and get into all kinds of scrapes, or else to suffer and be unhappy. They don't know that they have been sent to work as labourers on a building site, that their mission is to manifest and give concrete expression on earth to the divine element within them, to become like God Himself — but here, on earth. In the world above, matter is so subtle that it obeys the impulse of thought, imagination and will instantaneously; you can do anything with it. Yes, but if man remained in those subtle regions where creative work is so easy, he would not be obliged to grow and develop all his possibilities. This is why he has been sent into the world: to permeate the crude, opaque matter of earth with the beauty and splendour of God.

We are told that the Lord created Heaven and earth at the same time, and this holds a lesson for us: since He created them together, it means that it is not only Heaven that is important. The earth, too, is important and must be organized and made beautiful so that it shall be like Heaven. Heaven and earth must match perfectly. At the moment, this is not the case. The earth — by which I mean the world of men — does not vibrate in harmony, in tune with the divine world. When man becomes con-

scious of the mission he has been sent to accomplish, he will begin
to take care of the world; that is to say, his whole being will begin
to vibrate in unison with the vibrations of the divine world and
then, at last, he will reflect the beauty, light and intelligence of
the world above. Only then will he have accomplished his mission. And as the earth, that is to say the planet on which we are
living, corresponds to our physical bodies, it too will be transformed and become subtle, vibrant and luminous and will produce other fruits, other plants and flowers. When human beings
understand that their work starts with themselves, when they begin
to change their own body and brain, everything else will change
too. Then the earth will truly be the receptacle of Heaven.

Once they have accomplished their task, human beings will
be free to leave the earth and go to other planets, other regions.
Yes, once they have done their work; not before. So many suffering human beings long to leave this earth, this 'vale of tears'!
To be sure, there is a great deal of suffering and unhappiness
here on earth but where does it come from and who is to blame?
Human beings. In any case, the fact that you suffer is not sufficient reason to leave the field of battle and run away. Heaven
cannot tolerate deserters. You will say, 'But I long for Paradise,
for Heavenly beatitude; I long for peace and light and beauty!'
I realize that and, of course, you will be given credit for it, for
it is a positive quality. But it is not enough: the work is still waiting
to be done; you haven't completed your task.

The matter of this earth is so coarse and opaque that it is going to take millions of years and millions of human beings to
transform it. And how can we transform it? By eating it. This
is another thing that science has never really understood: why
we eat. We eat earth. Oh, of course, it doesn't look like earth
because it is in the form of fruit and vegetables, but it is still earth,
and it has to go through us and be swallowed, digested and
eliminated... swallowed, digested and eliminated, over and over
again, until it is imbued with the emanations and vibrations produced by our thoughts and feelings. Once the earth is thoroughly

impregnated in this way it will have become so subtle that it will be the Kingdom of God. One day the earth will be luminous and transparent because, as it goes through us, it gives us something of itself but it also receives something from us, something of our thoughts and feelings, something of our vitality; already the earth is not the same as it was in the remote past. It has evolved a great deal and is much subtler and more intelligent because all the human beings who have ever lived on the planet have worked to change it.

Evolution, the transformation of matter, is what life is all about. Exactly what forms and manifestations we shall see in the future is another question, but there is a reason, a plan, a law that impels the whole of creation to evolve. This is why those who contribute to this evolution are helped and encouraged. Everything has to evolve. Even minerals evolve. The evolution of minerals is imperceptible but it is no less real; there is a force at work within them that will eventually allow them to manifest their inherent properties and virtues. The precious stones and metals which have healing, beneficial properties are the more highly evolved minerals. Plants also evolve and, the more they evolve, the more they produce flowers and fruit with beneficial curative and nutritious properties. The same is true of animals and also of men; it is even true of the whole solar system which is gradually moving towards the constellation of Hercules.

The law of life, therefore, is evolution, that is to say growth, development to the point of perfection. This is why Jesus said, 'You shall be perfect, just as your Father in Heaven is perfect'. But the question then arises of how we should understand perfection. Human beings have certain ideas on the subject; in every area they try to find the best, quickest, most accurate or most harmonious way of doing things. The only trouble is that they do not always have the right standards by which to judge and yet, if they were more observant, they would see that Cosmic Intelligence has placed models for our guidance all around us. The human body is one excellent example, for it is easy to recognize when it is functioning perfectly: if you eat and drink properly and breathe, sleep and work well, you say that your health is perfect. It is possible, therefore, to have some idea of what perfection means on the physical plane; on other planes, though, it is less easy to have any concept of perfection.

The whole question is extremely rich. One of the first things we see, if we look at it closely, is that there exists a law that obliges all beings to grow towards perfection and that anyone or anything that opposes this law has to suffer the consequences. Without realizing it, human beings often oppose this law. When they behave in a way that hinders the proper functioning of their physical body, for instance, they are preventing it from attaining perfect physical health. Or again, by a lack of intellectual work or warped thoughts, they hinder the development of the brain and let it lapse into darkness.

In the world above everything is perfect and it is up to us to work to establish that perfection in every area here, on earth.

Let's try to make this clearer by taking the example of a human being. For me, human beings have always been a key, a yardstick: in order to find the solution to a problem I look at human beings and find the solution in them. In this instance too, therefore, let's take the example of a human being: on the level of thought a human being is all-powerful: he can imagine, invent and organize wonderful things; it is only when it comes to giving those things concrete reality that he is at a loss. The facility that already exists in his mind still has to be brought down onto the material plane. Suppose, for example, that you are thinking of a very complicated dance step or a sequence in gymnastics: in your imagination you do it perfectly; your difficulties only begin when you try to execute it on the physical plane. You have to practise over and over again before you succeed. And the same is true of all activities: it is not enough to create things on the mental plane, you have to give them reality on the physical plane as well. The reason why we have descended to earth is to make manifest the glory and splendour of God, to give material reality to His power, intelligence and perfection.

This is just one example of how my observation of human beings helps me to solve this and many other problems. Try to do the same: when you have a problem try to use human beings as the key. You can still see ancient statues in Egypt that represent a Pharaoh holding a key that symbolized man and this means that the Pharaoh possessed the key to the universe – man – and could use that key to decipher all the riddles of the universe. I, too, possess that key. You will not see me standing on a pedestal holding a key in my hand but, if you were clairvoyant, you would have realized a long time ago that I possessed this key.

We have come into the world with a mission, therefore. But don't misunderstand this word 'mission'. A lot of very unexceptional people imagine that they have a special mission. It is quite astounding to see how some miserably puny, feeble people, who have no special gifts or faculties, get it into their heads that they have been sent to restore order on earth. It is true, of course, that we all have a mission, but it is very important to know what that mission is and not to delude ourselves. Our mission is to develop all the qualities and virtues that Heaven has sown in us as germs, seeds. It may well be that, from time to time, Heaven chooses a particular being for a particular mission, but the common mission of man is to grow and develop until he reaches perfection. All men, even if they have no great gifts, even if they are half-witted, have received this mission: to work, to become more and more perfect, to evolve. Unfortunately, there are always plenty of candidates for the false missions, plenty of people who think that, like Joan of Arc, they are going to save their country but who are not interested in their true mission. Don't imitate them, my dear brothers and sisters; start by concentrating on the mission that God has entrusted to all human beings: to become perfect as He is perfect. And, as one lifetime is too short to complete your task, you will come back again and go on with it in your next incarnation.

I have already explained that, when Jesus said, 'You shall be
perfect, just as your Father in Heaven is perfect', the fact of reincarnation was implicit[1], for how could someone as wise and
clear-sighted as Jesus expect human beings to become perfect in
the space of one lifetime? If there were no such thing as reincarnation this precept would be absurd, but in the light of reincarnation it becomes both understandable and possible. If Jesus asked
perfection of human beings it was precisely because he knew that
perfection was the law of the universe.

Everything in the universe has to advance, improve and evolve
and, when something or someone flouts this law, they are
destroyed: human civilizations, worlds, even constellations have
already vanished because they defied the law of evolution. In fact,
you would be amazed to know how many things in the universe
are continually being destroyed or disappearing while new things
are appearing. The human brain is still incapable of containing
the immensity of the universe.

From now on, therefore, make up your minds to take this
law of evolution seriously and tell yourselves that you must evolve,
you must make progress, otherwise you will find yourselves up
against the law. If you work in this spirit you will be restoring
order within yourselves, your whole life will be transformed and
you will create a magnificent future for yourselves. Unfortunately,
very few men and women are imbued with this idea; they work,
but the goal of their work is not perfection; on the contrary, they
work in order to dominate more people, acquire more possessions and have more pleasure. They don't work and study for
a divine idea. You can see proof of this in the fact that, once
they have got what they wanted for themselves, they work and
study no more. Yes, everybody works, but the goal for which
they work is always selfish.

Don't expect perfection to come from elsewhere. To promise
human beings that they will be given everything they want without

1 See *Complete Works*, vol 12, chap. 8, 'Reincarnation'.

having to make the slightest effort is to mislead them. In fact, if you always got everything you asked for, you would be unhappier than ever. Why? Because it would not have cost you any effort; it is when we strive for something that we are happiest. Look at the question of money: does someone who never worked to earn his money really appreciate it? No. Get it into your heads, therefore, that you have a mission and do everything in your power to accomplish it.

Sèvres, April 1, 1972

II

When someone feels that he is not very presentable — perhaps because his clothes are shabby or he is not feeling well — he avoids the company of others because he doesn't want to be seen like that. When he feels on top of his form, on the other hand, he wants others to see his radiance and be attracted to him and give him something — if only their approval. This is a perfectly natural reaction: all animals, even birds, have this instinct. They know what it means to be beautiful or ugly. Doesn't a peacock that has lost his gorgeous tail feathers keep out of sight? Whereas, at any other time, he struts about and shows them off. Everybody sees these things but they look no further than the outer reality. For my part, I go a step further; in fact, I will go so far as to say that if someone does not want to live in a brotherhood it is because he feels that he is not handsome enough, not inwardly beautiful. I assure you: this is absolutely true. When you are full of good feelings and overflowing with love you are eager to pour it out on others. And when you are drained and empty, you want to be alone to recuperate. If you like living in a brotherhood, therefore, it is a good sign and, if you always want to be alone in your own little corner, it is a very bad sign. Perhaps you have this attitude because you think that you are extremely intelligent.

That may be true, your intellect may be very highly developed, but it is on the psychic and emotional level that you are flawed and under-developed. I repeat: when someone is truly rich within himself he feels the need to share his wealth with others.

This means that all those who want to live in a brotherhood are welcome here. Even if they haven't got any very outstanding talents, as long as they emanate this brotherly love we shall give them all the rest. Yes, because this is the element we need in order to make the world a better place. Intellectual and artistic qualities alone will never make the world better. In fact, we have too much of these things today: too many intellectuals, too many scientists, too many artists and not enough people who love a life of brotherhood! Everything will be changed when human beings start to understand that it is brotherhood that will save the world, but that time has not yet come. They think that the solution to their problems lies in more education; nobody spares a thought for the collectivity, for the rest of the world; the personal, egotistical side of people is over-developed.

But you, at least, surely you can understand that, if you persist in isolating yourselves and working only for your own interests, you will not receive much help? You absolutely must get rid of the illusion that you will be happier and freer and more successful if you manage by yourself. It is not true: if you sing solo you will never achieve the tonal richness produced by a choir.

To be sure, history shows that human beings have understood at least one thing: that it was to their advantage to live together in groups. Without this they would still be at the stage of spending all their days hunting for food in the forest. As soon as men saw that it would be more practical to combine their forces, each individual benefited from the new situation: while some were fishing or hunting, others wove cloth or built their huts, etc. And so, today, everybody is at the service of everybody else and each individual benefits from all the advantages that this gives. It is thanks to this that man can progress. Each individual has his own, limited activity and all the rest is at his disposal: libraries, hospitals, public transport, police protection, etc., etc. None of that is possible if you live alone. It is thanks to this collaboration that man has been able to put his intelligence to work to acquire the means to change the world itself.

Unfortunately, man's intelligence is still not perfect because it has always been developed for reasons of self-interest. Everybody benefits from the extraordinary progress that has been made, but only externally. Inwardly, they are still isolated and apart; they are not united. Outwardly, it is true, the individual members of nations and societies help and support each other through institutions of national defence, social security, family allowances, etc. But man has still not understood what this progress in objective realities means. He has still not deciphered the message contained in all the facilities, possibilities and advantages of modern life nor transposed them onto the plane of his own inner life. There is still a lot of work to do, therefore, in order to form this inner society, this human community on the spiritual plane. Inwardly, human beings are still apart and mutually hostile; they are not moving together towards the same goal. Without realizing it, the different countries are working for separation, isolation. Of course, they have various forms of international relations that go by such names as Ministry of Foreign Affairs, Diplomacy, Foreign Trade and so on but, in reality, each nation is determined to defend its separate identity, each one wants to be a world power and to impose its will on the others. No, truly, there are not many who are inwardly united. This is why we must work to make inner universal brotherhood a reality; we must work to unite human beings, peoples and nations and help them to attain that sublime consciousness of unity and a life of fulfilment and abundance, a life of inner prosperity.

Proof that this question is only half solved can be seen in the fact that, although human beings have achieved fantastic results on the outer level, on the inner level they are still tormented and unhappy, they still feel cold, empty, poor and in darkness. This shows that progress has to be taken a stage further. Outwardly, most people have food and lodging. Even the very poor, even beggars, are given shelter and looked after when they are ill; something is being done, even for the most destitute. External conditions, therefore, are far better than in the past. Yes, but what about man's inner conditions? This is the work of the future: to procure an inner prosperity for humanity equal to that it enjoys outwardly.

What is preventing human beings from forming the Great Universal White Brotherhood, from being truly brothers and sisters? What is preventing them? I have told you: an illusion. The illusion that they will be much happier alone. Yes, but the years go by and they find that, on the contrary, they are less happy. When you are alone there is no one to help and support you. Look at an unmarried schoolteacher: if she were always alone she would become a dried-up old maid but the children are there and she has to teach them; without realizing it, she draws life from her contact with them; she is nourished and rejuvenated by their emanations. When you see a teacher like that, so full of love and sweetness, you don't know whom you would most like to hug: the children or their teacher. She's so adorable that sometimes – quite by accident I assure you – it's the teacher you hug!

Every individual must be free to live his own life. That is normal; no one is going to ask you to let yourself be absorbed into the lives of others. You have your own life, your own organism; you are separate and independent, but you must be one with others in the invisible world. The different cells of your body are not all merged into one: a heart cell is different from a stomach cell, each has its own individuality, but the ties and affinities that hold them together create the state of harmony that we call health. Is that so difficult to understand? Nobody is going to ask a black man to become white or a white man to become yellow. No one is going to ask a Muslim to become a Buddhist or a Buddhist to become a Christian (although the Christians have always sent missionaries to convert Indians, Africans and Asians. In most cases, however, the results were not good). Everyone must be allowed to keep his own characteristics, therefore, but their mutual understanding must be such that it welds them into one in the divine world.

This is why, I assure you, the Universal White Brotherhood is unique in that it alone is not a sect. Its Teaching embraces all human beings and is founded on universal truths found in the traditions of ancient Egypt and India, Persia, Greece and Israel. Even if I have to be burnt at the stake for it, I must declare loud and clear, before all the Bishops and Cardinals of the Church: 'You have turned Christianity into a sect. At the beginning it was a universal religion but now, through ignorance and because you have pursued your own selfish interests, you have made it a sect. It no longer embraces all human beings, all our brothers and sisters, and it rejects many eternal truths.'

If you meditate on what I have been saying, you will understand how important it is to open your hearts and minds in order to have better possibilities for exchange with others. This is the spirit of the Universal White Brotherhood: to reach out to others, to create bonds of love, to give a helping hand, to embrace the whole world and feel that we are all members of the same family. Human beings are used to closing their doors to others, to going off alone and shutting themselves up in their own little corner. They don't realize that this philosophy is extremely pernicious, for they cannot receive any of the subtle elements that exist in such profusion unless they are open. All the blessings of Heaven are there, ready to pour into them, but they receive nothing because they have shut themselves up in their shells and slammed the door. And then they complain, 'No one hears me; no one ever comes to help me; Angels don't exist; God doesn't exist!' They put themselves in the worst possible situation and then they draw false conclusions from it.

As soon as a person succeeds in opening himself and communicating with the divine entities all around him, he realizes that they have always been there; that it was his own attitude that made it impossible to receive their help. Yes, because it is man's attitude that determines whether or not he receives the help he needs. He doesn't realize that, by shutting himself up in his selfishness, he is hurting himself and that he must learn to open himself, to reach out and love all creatures. This is what you learn in this Teaching: how to open yourselves. And you will see that, as soon as you open yourself, however slightly, you will be seized by a tremendous sense of wonder as you feel the divine blessings that surround you and flood over you and into you.

If insects have not evolved for billions of years, it is because they have never been willing to accept the point of view of those who were more advanced. They always say, 'No, no. The only truth is what we ourselves think and see and feel'. Oh, of course, I know you won't find this definition of an insect in a book of Natural History but that doesn't matter; I give it to you all the same: an insect is a creature who is a prisoner of his own point of view, his own ideas and his own self-interest. There is no changing him: he has his own opinion and nothing is going to shake him out of it. That is why he remains an insect.

A great many members of the Brotherhood still listen to the lectures and study the Teaching for their own sakes, not because they want to serve the ideal of the Teaching, to serve humanity. They have still not understood that their first reason for being here should be to break open the thick shell in which they encased themselves hundreds of years ago, and become capable not only of receiving the treasures that are all round them but also of distributing them to others. They are there in such profusion: it is not possible to keep them all for oneself! Believe me, many brothers and sisters have still not understood the real reason for our Teaching. They behave as though it were there only for their own enrichment. If you want to make progress, therefore, there is only one way, one method, and that is to become simple and natural, to be full of love and kindness and, above all, to share the benefits of all these divine elements you have received with others.

It is difficult, I know, and, for the moment, we are almost alone. But it is when things are difficult that we have to show Heaven that we are faithful and true. When there are already a lot of people who understand how necessary this attitude is, it will be less meritorious. It is now, when conditions are so difficult, that there is merit in becoming a model, an example for others. One day, if God gives me the opportunity to talk to the whole world, I shall say only this: 'All of you without exception, rich or poor, learned or ignorant, are entangled in inextricable difficulties simply because you do not know where your best interest lies. When it is a question of making a profit, amusing yourselves or waging war you are all there, without hesitation. But when it is a question of creating the conditions that would enable the whole of mankind to live happily, nobody moves. This means that you do not know where your own best interest lies. You don't really want to be happy; if you did you would all unite to make it possible.'

I assure you, when material goods, money or real estate are concerned, everybody is immediately ready and willing to contribute all their energies. But when it is a question of the happiness, freedom and fulfilment of the whole of mankind they are not interested. How can you explain this? Once human beings understand this one thing: where their own best interest lies, all their problems will be solved. To tell the truth, the question is perfectly clear and simple; it is just that nobody ever stops to think about it. They have to be told, 'If you have so many misfortunes and difficulties today, it is because you have asked for them. Consciously or unconsciously you have wished them on yourself. If you had wished for the opposite you would have it today.'

If everybody believed me and accepted what I am saying, the Kingdom of God would be established in this world in no time at all. But nobody accepts what I say; they are all determined to cling to their old ideas and traditions, their old attitudes, and this could go on for a very long time. Isn't this proof enough that human beings don't know where their best interest lies? But

I know it: it is in the Universal White Brotherhood, the whole of humanity becoming one family in which everyone loves, respects and helps the others and in which the billions now spent on destruction are used to help the poor, for it is poverty that encourages crime. But, as I say, human beings are so blind and false-hearted that they never see where their interest lies. Nothing you can say will make me believe that this is not so; I am firmly convinced of it: I have seen with my own eyes that human beings do not know their best interest. They continue to be evil, unjust and cruel; they continue to make life Hell, whereas it could be truly wonderful in no time at all.

There are two ways of looking at this question of your interest. The first is to think that you will be well off if you concentrate on your own affairs and forget about all the rest. The only trouble is that this is impossible: we are all part of the collective whole and if misfortune strikes we cannot hope to be spared. We shall be caught in the same storm as everybody else. Our private well-being, therefore, can never last long. The other way of looking at it — the only true way — is to think of the collective aspect and understand that the well-being or distress of the individual depends on the state of the collectivity. You must take a lesson from Nature: she gives air, light, warmth and food to the whole of humanity and lets each individual take what suits him.

Anyone who wants to promote his own interests to the detriment of the collectivity is a brainless fool who has never learned to reason, for the misfortunes of the collectivity will necessarily be his, too. As a member of the collectivity, whether he likes it or not, when disaster strikes he will go under with everybody else. When the collectivity is prosperous, on the other hand, each individual shares in its prosperity. This is how Cosmic Intelligence has ordained things, but human beings constantly work in opposition to Cosmic Intelligence: they grab everything for themselves and leave nothing for their neighbours. Well, this can last for a little while, but no one has ever survived for long by means of egoism, injustice and cruelty.

None of this is difficult to understand, but what counts is that people must want to change the situation and, unfortunately, they don't. They spend all their energy on their own interests − and perhaps a little on those of their family − and this will never solve our problems. How can humanity be made to understand that the Kingdom of God could be established within a few days? If the Brotherhood had many more members it would be very powerful and it could take things in hand and improve the situation. Look at the way political parties become strong: their members are united around an idea, that's all. And this is what makes them powerful. And what about us? Couldn't we do as much: couldn't we unite for this one goal, this one idea?

Even if we did nothing but unite around this one idea of the Kingdom of God it would be extraordinary. But we have all kinds of activities and, in spite of all those activities, the results are very meagre because the brothers and sisters are not really convinced. Whereas, in a political party, the members join forces and commit themselves for the sake of an idea, and there you are! Inwardly they may have all kinds of passions, vices and lusts but they are united by an idea. So why can't you, my dear brothers and sisters − you who have the benefit of a sublime Teaching and, above all, the idea of the Universal White Brotherhood − why can't you devote all your energies to that idea? Naturally, it is far easier to belong to a political party because it does not involve any great inner effort. But think of how these things often end: after a few years, the ruling party loses power and you find yourself in prison or in front of a firing squad. Really, human beings are too stupid! They give their lives unthinkingly for a political regime that cannot last, but when it is a question of working for something that could last for ever, nobody is willing to commit themselves. Nothing could be more stupid! If ever I exposed this stupidity in detail to the general public I would be banished from the country. No one would be able to deny the truth of it but they would find that truth too uncomfortable.

One day, you too will understand that human beings don't

know where their best interest lies. They believe that they will find it in things which, in fact, only serve to weaken and limit them. They need more light, therefore, and that light can only come from those who have studied and suffered and learned to recognize these truths. To be sure, the goal cannot be achieved overnight; it requires time and effort, but that doesn't matter; what matters is to know that our interest lies in reaching out, with our whole being, to that Heavenly goal and, if we have to endure some suffering on the way, that is not important. What is important is to keep advancing towards the very best that exists. That is where your own best interest lies.

The Bonfin, August 11, 1963

III

If it seems utterly impossible to us that the whole world should form one family, it is because we base our judgement on the external aspects of humanity. Outwardly, it is true, human beings are very different in the colour of their skin, in build, customs, culture and religion. If you tried to get Parisians and Eskimos to live together, the Parisians in Lapland and the Eskimos in Paris, you would have endless problems. If you look at the question more closely, however, you will understand that all human beings are inwardly alike. Above, in the Heavenly regions, they are all built on the same pattern with the same organs, the same capacities and needs, the same desires and the same ideal. But, as they don't live and know each other on that higher level, they cannot see that they are identical. When they look at each other down here, on the lower level, they cannot see that they are brothers and sisters; on the contrary, they feel so foreign and different, antagonistic even, that they often start to massacre each other.

As human beings evolve they will gradually know each other better and see that, inwardly, they are all alike: they all aspire to joy, happiness and freedom, to knowledge and light, and they all experience suffering in the same way. When they see this, they will begin to realize that it is only on the outside that they are different, that they are wearing different masks. They are like the members of a theatrical company: they fight and kill each other on stage, but in real life they are great friends. Human beings are all actors in a comedy — or a tragedy — but in real life they are brothers and sisters. If the countries that are at war with each other in the world today suddenly became aware that they all belonged to the one, Heavenly homeland, they would stop massacring each other. But this consciousness has not yet made itself felt. Human beings still live on too low a level, on the level of self-interest, concupiscence and greed. They are still not aware that they are all the sons and daughters of the same Father and Mother, the Heavenly Father and the Divine Mother; when they become conscious of this they will behave differently.

You must reflect and study until you reach this truth: that the more you know human beings on the higher level, the more it becomes apparent that they are all built on the same pattern and have the same needs; their differences are only external. But it is because of these differences that they are disunited. If you feel alien and isolated from others it is not possible to love them. But if you develop inwardly, if you awaken the sense of unity within you, you will begin to feel exactly what others feel. When human beings finally come to accept that their souls and spirits are united in the world above, they will form one immense family, the family of the Universal White Brotherhood; then they will automatically stop waging war on each other.

Actually, as I have already told you, I should say that war will never disappear; it will simply manifest itself differently. One day, all war will be a war of love; like the stars, human beings will bombard each other with rays of love. Yes, for just as there is a constant interchange of light between the constellations and suns in the heavens, the more highly evolved one is, the more light and love one exchanges with others. When I was very young, in Bulgaria, I often slept out under the stars, high up in the mountainous country above the Rila lakes, at an altitude of about 2,000 or 2,500 metres. Sometimes it would snow in the night and I would wake up wrapped in snow. What beautiful memories I have of that time! I would gaze and gaze at the stars until I fell asleep, and this was how I discovered that the stars were at war with each other and that their weapons were rays of light. And I understood that, one day, human beings would also 'fight' each other with rays of love and light and colour. Cosmic Intelligence will never take away man's need to make war; it is only the forms of war that will change: in the future, men will no longer make war with bombs and cannons but with rays of love, light and colour. And it will be total war. I'm all in favour of that kind of war; in fact, I have personally declared war on the whole of humanity. There is nothing more marvellous than this kind of war!

There are certain elements and tendencies in human nature which can never be changed but they must all be made to converge towards the same point, the summit. Look at the pyramids; a pyramid is a symbol which teaches us that everything must converge towards one goal, the highest point, the Prime Cause, the Lord. As long as things are always separate and divergent there can be no lasting peace. Human beings must be given a different philosophy, a Teaching such as ours, then peace will be possible.

It has been said, 'Man, know thyself'. Yes, man must know himself as he is outwardly but also as he is inwardly. And this is just the point: inwardly there is no difference between men; whatever their race or their level of civilization, they have all been created and fashioned on the same pattern in the Lord's workshops. For the time being, as they are too deeply sunk into matter, they cannot help but hate each other; it is impossible for them to do anything else. If you look at the creatures that live in swamps and jungles, you will see that they all devour each other; but if you look at those that live on a much higher level, amongst the angelic hierarchies, you will see that they do nothing but embrace each other and exchange gifts. Yes, in the higher regions they exchange love whilst down below they exchange hatred and hostility. This is why human beings, who have sunk to such a low level, cannot do otherwise than devour each other. But then they draw the conclusion that man will always devour his fellow man and that the law of the jungle prevails in the world. This will be true as long as you persist in living on the lowest levels, but the higher you go the more love you will find. Go all the way up to the sun and you will find such love... nothing but love. If human beings could reach high enough they would be so dazzled, so full of wonder at the reality they perceive, that they would immediately reach out the hand of friendship to each other and the Golden Age would be upon us.

There, I am obliged to say it again: without the light of the Teaching that the Universal White Brotherhood brings, we shall never achieve anything. With it, everything becomes possible. There are already a few men and women in the world who have understood and are working in this direction but, as they have no influence with the people in charge, the latter continue to do as they please and the sorry plight of the world remains unchanged. But in the long run, if we persevere with our work and are truly united, truly one, we shall undermine the power of those who rule with cruelty and injustice and they will be forced to change. Yes, we have to force them, not at the point of a gun, of course, not with threats or arms, with nothing but the power of light... but we must force them, all the same. If we were very numerous they would have to take us into account. In the face of such light, such love and harmony, they would all capitulate.

We have every right to win our battles, but our only weapons must be the power of light, the power of the spirit and of love. Nothing is ever achieved by rebellions or massacres. It doesn't take long for things to be even worse than before. Personally, I am a revolutionary; no one is more revolutionary than I am, but my methods are different. Very quickly, after every revolution, the same disorder, the same corruption and waste, the same injustice is rampant again. Victims and executioners have changed sides, that's all... but there are still victims and there are still executioners. So where is the improvement? Genuine improvement can never be obtained by changing things externally. It is the mentality of human beings that needs to be changed; revolution must take place in men's minds. And that is where I can make it take place: if I have enough workers with me, those who misuse their power will be forced to disappear and Heaven will replace them with true servants of the light.

Try to understand me, therefore, and to do everything in your power to propagate the Teaching so that the whole world may benefit from it. To be sure, a great many people today are working for the well-being and happiness of mankind and for world peace but, as their understanding of these things is too materialistic, their work is largely futile. True progress, true change, takes place in the mind, in the heart and soul, and it takes place thanks to light. Nothing will ever truly be changed as long as men cling to the same selfish, dishonest, deceitful mentality. How can reforms be effective if the mentality is still the same? It is when the mentality is changed that society will automatically change. Everything depends on people's mentality, and mentalities can only be changed by a new philosophy. Try to give me a helping hand and you will see what we can accomplish together. I hardly need to give you examples when I say that there are always thousands who are ready to demonstrate and shout and scream in support of the most outlandish and idiotic ideas but never more than a handful ready to support the best ideas, our idea. This is what makes me say that human beings don't know where their true interest lies. They are ready to spill their blood for an idea that is utterly stupid, but not a drop will they spare for the Kingdom of God!

I know human nature: I know what human nature is on the lowest level and what it is on the highest level. As long as you know only the lower nature of man you can truthfully say that he is a wild beast. But you must look deeper and recognize the divinity hidden within him, then you will see that the wild beasts can be made to give way to Angels. Human beings have lived on the level of their selfish instincts and passions for too long and, naturally, this has not left much room for manifestations of magnanimity, nobility and generosity. It is true that there are wild beasts in man; you only have to scratch the surface or deprive him of something and you will see how promptly he strikes back if he has made no effort to be nobler or more enlightened. But as soon as he begins to control and spiritualize himself he is capable of rising above such small-mindedness.

Let me tell you a story: there was once a kingdom that was constantly plagued by disease and famine and every kind of misfortune. At his wit's end to know what to do about it, the king of that country consulted a sage. The wise man told him: 'Your Majesty, it is you who are the cause of all these misfortunes. It is because you live a life of debauchery and are cruel and unjust that your subjects are visited by so many calamities.' Then, leaving the king's presence, the sage stood up before the people and told them: 'If you suffer, it is because you deserve to: you have called this tyrant upon yourselves by the senseless way you live.' This is the explanation of the sages and, when we know this law, we can understand that, when the people of a country improve, Heaven sends them enlightened rulers who bring them well-being and prosperity but, when they sink into evil ways, Heaven sends a tyrant to rule over them. This is the law. It is important to know that there are laws.

When the population of a country decides to live according to the light, Heaven sends them rulers of nobility and integrity and the country is blessed. But if a population finds itself ruled by despots against whom there is no appeal, they must know that it is their own fault. Why was Bulgaria occupied for several centuries by the Turks? Because, instead of listening to the Bogomils, they massacred them and drove them out of the country. Then came centuries of darkness... the Turks invaded Bulgaria and oppressed its people for five hundred years. When a country drives out the light it pays dearly for it in the form of all kinds of misfortunes. I assure you, although people rarely see the connection, this is a law. You must never reject the light for, sooner or later, you will pay the penalty. If you don't believe me, go and verify this for yourselves in the historical records of the cosmos. The laws are implacable. People imagine that they can transgress them at will and it is true that they can do so for a while but, in the long run, they always have to pay for their defiance. This is why it is so important that people should know this law, especially those who rule ; but ordinary citizens also. And they must realize that if they are ruled by a tyrant they are only getting what they deserve ; he has been sent to them by the Invisible World.

This is why you must accept the light I bring you and learn to live properly. In this way you will attract enlightened, clear-sighted rulers who are well versed in human nature and know how the universe is constructed and understand the laws that govern it.

The Bonfin, August 21, 1971

IV

What a marvellous climate of silence, harmony and love! This is the atmosphere that gives you the best possible conditions in which to find peace and serenity and communion with luminous entities. These are the moments I love best. Of course, I can and do enjoy such moments when I am at home alone, but I would rather do so with you. When we are all together in this ambience of brotherly love, each one contributes something of his own, something special. Ours is a special kind of restaurant because you have to bring your own food with you. Not on the material level, of course, but on the spiritual level; each one brings a dish, some fruit from his garden or field, something from his soul, a fluid, an emanation, a quality that all can share and enjoy. Instead of remaining alone with nothing but your radishes or tomatoes — because that is the only thing that grows in your garden, symbolically speaking — you can share all kinds of delicious dishes brought by all the other generous brothers and sisters: patience, gentleness, strength, health, love, tenderness, purity, intelligence, faith, hope and so on. What a banquet!

This is the great secret of the Brotherhood: if you remain alone you will always be poor whereas, in the Brotherhood, there is an abundance to be shared and enjoyed. When you are feeling discouraged, for instance, you will see joy or serenity on other people's faces and, without realizing it, you receive some particles of their peace and gaiety and begin to take heart again. If you remain alone you can never be enriched in this way; in fact, you will become continually poorer for, when one stops growing richer one inevitably grows poorer. But in a collective, brotherly way of life everyone gains, and gains immensely, for Heaven distributes its riches to us through the intermediary of other human beings. Once you understand this you will no longer be able to do without the Brotherhood.

For my part, it is quite clear to me that, although I can pray and meditate alone, at home, I prefer it when we do so together. What about you? Do you feel the same? Yes, I can see that you do. This year, more than in previous years, I can sense that you have understood that your happiness is to be found in this atmosphere of the Brotherhood, that it is in this ambience that you blossom and become freer. Many people are reluctant to join a Brotherhood because they are afraid of losing their freedom, their individuality. They don't realize that it is in the ordinary world that people lose their individuality. In the ordinary world people all copy each other, they all quarrel, they are all unhappy. Whereas here, when you accept the collective way of life, the result is extraordinary, you become much freer and more independent, much more yourselves. You begin to hold up your head because you find that you are extremely well equipped for magnificent achievements. Tell me honestly: do you really feel stifled and diminished here? Or do you feel, on the contrary, that you are growing wings? Oh, I know: some people are so peculiar that even if you took them to the very threshold of Paradise they would have the gravest misgivings about going in.

Tell me, what do you think about this ambience? And it is you yourselves that have created it. In the past I had to do all the work, all alone, to create such an ambience, and now it is you who create it. The silence that reigns while we meditate is no longer only external; something has changed inwardly as well.

There is a harmony and sweetness that was not there before; I can feel it. Before, even when all was quiet externally, I could hear the din of your thoughts and feelings but, now, peace is beginning to reign even in your inner thoughts and feelings. So, let me rejoice in this and congratulate you! Keep up the good work and, one day, we shall produce such powerful and harmonious vibrations that many friends will come from Heavenly regions and walk amongst us, bringing us their glorious colours and scents and music. You are thinking, 'What on earth is he talking about? Does he really expect me to believe all that? No one has ever told us anything like it!' Well, now I am telling you and, if you believe me and work as I tell you, it will not be long before you will see these entities coming to visit us.

Some of you will object, 'Yes, but even here, in the Brotherhood, there are any number of people I find very unattractive'. Of course you do! But that doesn't matter; even if you don't find everybody to your taste, at least there is an exchange going on between you and the collectivity and that is preferable to remaining isolated. Just as it is preferable to suffer rather than to remain as insensate as a stone. At least, when you suffer, you learn something and your suffering awakens and develops forces within you; you cannot develop if you never feel anything. Initiates and Sages have always chosen to face up to difficulties because they know that, by accepting their sufferings and difficulties gladly, they will evolve more rapidly.

Most human beings don't know these truths and they think that, once they have chosen the most sublime ideal, the ideal of perfection, they should be able to achieve it without having to experience states that are directly contrary to it. But that is impossible. And it is essential that you realize that it is impossible, otherwise the first little difficulty will discourage you. Are you wondering why everything does not immediately become marvellous, since your only goal is the good and the Kingdom of God and His Righteousness? The reason is that we always have

to tread a path sown with snares and obstacles before we can reach
our goal; even Jesus had to go through Hell before reaching his
Father in Heaven. And before you can attain the Sephirah
Tiphareth (the Sun) on the Sephirotic Tree, you have to pass
through Yesod (the Moon), whose lower region accumulates and
condenses everything evil[2]. Yes, when you want to attain
Heaven you begin to be attacked by Hell, for it is not possible
to achieve a divine, luminous ideal all at once, without suffering
and struggling. If someone does so, if he carries out a divine,
grandiose scheme at once, it means that he has already known
great suffering and worked very hard in his previous incarnations
and now, in this incarnation, he has the qualities required to succeed immediately.

The fact that you are going to meet contradictions and difficulties along the way does not mean that you should not continue to strive towards the world of harmony and light. The
obstacles in your way are no reason for renouncing your ideal
for, however painful they may be, they are only temporary. One
day you will free yourself from them and, when that day comes,
you will enjoy an eternal state of fulfilment. So, in spite of all
the trials you have to endure, it is well worth continuing on the
path that leads to joy, happiness, freedom, splendour, perfection and fulfilment.

As long as we are on this earth, obstacles, conflict and suffering cannot be avoided; no one is exempt, not even the divine
beings that have incarnated in order to help mankind. The only
difference is that these exceptional beings had a different attitude.
They were not spared the difficulties experienced by others, but
they rose above them and used all obstacles to go further and
climb higher, to reach the summit, whereas others turn back or
are defeated and annihilated. This is the only difference. But there
are no exceptions to the rule. The sons of God encounter just

2 See *Complete Works*, vol. 7, the lecture entitled 'The River of Life'.

as many obstacles in life as the sons of the earth: it is our common lot. The important thing is to have the right attitude, to know how to understand your difficulties and how to react to them. It is people's attitude, the way they understand and react to circumstances, that makes them great or small. If you want to become great, never let yourself dream that you will, one day, have no more difficulties and obstacles to contend with. This state of affairs will endure until mankind is transformed and the Golden Age is established amongst men. Until then, we shall always find obstacles in our path for it is a collective problem. Certain problems can be resolved only if the whole collectivity decides to change.

Gandhi's philosophy of non-violence is a good example of this. At the specific moment in history and in the specific circumstances in which it flourished, it was magnificent. And it made it possible for India to free itself from the British. But, generally speaking, non-violence is a dangerous doctrine; if a country is alone in practising it, it runs the risk of being swallowed up. Non-violence is the ideal solution only if the whole of mankind adopts the same philosophy.

Actually, Gandhi was not the first to preach the philosophy of non-violence. Jesus advocated non-violence, for instance, when he said, 'Whoever slaps you on your right cheek, turn the other to him also'[3], and, when he himself was arrested and beaten, he did not try to hit back. Jesus was the perfect manifestation of non-violence; he wanted to give an example that all men could imitate one day, but he knew very well that if this philosophy was practised by only a few individuals or nations, it would be dangerous: there would always be cruel and selfish neighbours who would hasten to wipe out the poor wretches who refused to defend themselves. Jesus bequeathed this philosophy to his disciples so that they, in turn, might give an example by paying

3 See *Complete Works*, vol. 12, chap. 20 for a fuller explanation of this text.

with their lives. And this is exactly what many saints and martyrs did and, in so doing, hastened their own evolution: they paid their debts and freed themselves from the bonds of karma and, in this way, they were able to return to earth with exceptional gifts and possibilities.

Non-violence is an excellent philosophy for someone who wants to conquer his personality and evolve more rapidly, but it cannot solve the problem of war in the world. A nation that decided not to defend itself would very soon be wiped out both economically and physically.

The only solution, therefore, is for the philosophy of non-violence to become collective. Instead of remaining an ideal in the minds of a few Initiates and spiritualists[4], it must be adopted by the whole of mankind for, until it becomes collective, it will never change anything. Think of all the people who have wanted to give an example of nobility only to be assassinated! Did their sacrifice change humanity in any way? No. So, these ideas have to be adopted in every country in the world. An attitude that can be good when it is collective can be dangerous if it is held by only a few. But, although the philosophy of non-violence may be dangerous when it remains purely individual, it is still something positive, for those who sacrifice their lives in this way come back to earth with extraordinary gifts, thanks to which they can influence others in the right direction. The question of non-violence must find a global solution, otherwise it will always be a problem.

Sèvres, April 1, 1963

---

4 The word 'spiritualist', in the language of Omraam Mikhaël Aïvanhov, means one who looks at things from a spiritual point of view, whose philosophy of life is based on belief in a spiritual reality.

V

The Master reads the Meditation for the day:

'When you are meditating in silence, learn to link yourself to the life of the collectivity. The one word that has the deepest significance in the spiritual life is 'unity'. Unity teaches a disciple how to live a collective way of life; it is the Alpha and Omega of esoteric science. All the high Initiates begin and end their teaching with this idea of unity, union, union with the universe and with God.'

Union with the universe; union with God... Yes, that is what we are talking about, although many people today claim that God doesn't exist and, in doing so, think they are showing how intelligent they are. Well, there may be some idiots to admire them, but they will not be admired by Initiates. To be sure, everyone has the right to believe or not to believe, but an unbeliever has no right to persuade others not to believe. We always have the right to bring others closer to the Lord, to enlighten them and help them to improve, to heal them and make them happy and free, but we have no right to plunge them into darkness, to spread confusion and doubt in their minds. Nowadays, everybody − particularly

the young – think they can do whatever they please. They can...
you can. That's true. But I don't recommend it because the consequences are terrible: the evil you do will turn back on you and
wipe you out. In the same way, the good you do comes back to
you multiplied a hundredfold. Everything is permitted, but beware
of the consequences! Do something dangerous as an experiment,
from time to time, if you really want to, in this way you will get
to know the laws and learn how dependable they are, but devote
the whole of your energies and all your thoughts and feelings to
good.

   This question of the existence or non-existence of God is really
quite simple. For someone who does not believe in God, God does
not exist, for it depends on us whether something exists or not.
Look at a man who is asleep: the treasures of the whole world
can be piled up beside him but, as he is not aware of them, he
is incapable of taking pleasure in them. Almost all human beings are like that man: they are plunged into an unconscious sleep.
Only Initiates are truly awake; only they can see and delight in
the splendour of all the treasures around them. Others live in the
midst of exactly the same treasures but are unaware of them, so
they never stop complaining and moaning and weeping because
they have no wife or no house or not enough money. Men have
been put to sleep by matter, by pleasure, by their futile activities
and this is why the Invisible World tries to shake them from their
sleep, every now and then, by sending them a few calamities, a
war or some other misfortune. When this happens, of course,
they wake up for a little while, but they soon go back to sleep
again. We read that Jesus' disciples slept even in the Garden of
Gethsemane; he asked them to 'watch and pray', but they fell
asleep and left him to watch alone.

   Everything depends on our state of consciousness. When we
are awake, certain things become reality and then, when we go
to sleep, they fade away. And this is what happens with God:
when we are asleep we are unaware of Him and say that He
doesn't exist.

The passage I read to you a moment ago underlines the importance of the life of the community. Someone who refuses to participate in the collective life does not realize how much he is limiting himself. He lives within the narrow confines of his own desires, appetites and feelings without a thought for others, and this is a great poverty. It is a state that is normal for a child, but a child grows up and this means that he begins to take an interest in someone else: he marries and the circle expands slightly. Gradually, some little 'visitors' arrive and his circle expands again, but it is still very limited. It must expand more and more until it includes his country, his race, the whole of mankind and even more, until it reaches beyond all boundaries to immensity, infinity. But only Initiates are capable of transcending all boundaries and limitations; all their aspirations, all their thoughts and interests, all their efforts converge in the direction of the collectivity, the universal dimension of life.

And now let me add this: all the spiritual movements in the world today are wonderful and necessary; they are all seeking knowledge, power and realization, and this is right and good. The only thing is that they still do not enjoy the expanded consciousness that would free them from too great a preoccupation, as in the past, with the salvation of the individual, and allow them to be more concerned with the collective dimension. It is right for men to aspire to knowledge and power but only in order to use them as a means towards the much higher goal of brotherhood and a universal life. History contains numerous examples of people who had great gifts, particularly the gifts of healing and clairvoyance, but who used their gifts exclusively for their own enrichment or prestige; they were not interested in using them to promote the Kingdom of God and universal brotherhood and this is why, in spite of the gifts and powers they enjoyed, they were never truly contented. But those who work for the collectivity, for the ideal of universality, are always overflowing with happiness even if they have no special gifts or powers.

Believe me, my dear brothers and sisters, if you devote all your

energies, all your strength to this work of the Initiates for a divine
goal, you will always feel happy and fulfilled even if you are alone.
By dedicating yourself to this work you are reinforcing the egregor
of the Universal White Brotherhood. Every religious, political
or cultural movement forms an egregor. Every country, too. An
egregor is a psychic being formed by the thoughts, desires and
fluidic emanations of all its members who are working together
towards the same goal. In the world above, the egregors of different collectivities are often at war with each other and some
clairvoyants can see these conflicts. Each egregor has its own form
and colour: the egregor of France, for example, is a cock, that
of Russia a bear, and so on. But neither the cock nor the bear
nor the dragon can give the world what it needs. The time has
come for the whole of mankind to unite in forming the egregor
of the dove, for it is the dove that brings peace. But who will
do this if people work only for themselves? Will Christians? Look
at Ireland and see what Catholics and Protestants are working
for: for their own little ideology... and the destruction of all
others. And wherever you look you see the same conflicts.

The Universal White Brotherhood has made its appearance
because the spirits above have decided to introduce a new current amongst human beings. You will say that there are already
so many spiritual groups: the Rosicrucians, the Theosophists, An-
throposophists, Mazdaznans and Knights of Malta... not to mention the Trumpets of the Most High! Surely, that's enough? No,
it's not enough, because nothing very marvellous has resulted from
all this. Each group works for itself, for its own little clan; each
one behaves as though it were the hub of the universe and believes
that it, and it alone, possesses the truth. In fact, it would be true
to say that it is the spiritual movements that are obstructing the
establishment of the Kingdom of God. Their goal is to work for
good, for the light, but they are not working for the collectivity.
Only the Universal White Brotherhood accepts every single being with all his peculiarities. It doesn't claim to be superior to
the other movements in knowledge, virtue or power; I am not

narrow-minded, I know that they are magnificent and that they have all these things; I don't want to belittle them, but they lack the new element of warmth and love that we bring. I have attended meetings of many of the spiritual movements. They are cold, aloof and proud — and they will never bring about the Kingdom of God on earth with such an attitude. Here, in the Brotherhood, we may have only this one element, the spirit of brotherhood but, for the moment, it is what matters most. Human beings possess great knowledge, powers and wealth, but nobody is interested in acquiring the one thing that can make of the world one great family: the spirit of brotherhood. If more and more people make up their minds to work for the collective life and not only for their own power, prestige, glory or wealth, the Kingdom of God will be established on earth. It is not complicated: it is simply a question of working towards a different goal.

The true meaning of life is to participate in the work of our elder brothers, those great Spirits who want to help mankind, and to tell oneself, 'I want to change; I want to work for a divine idea'. In this way, this divine idea will grow and spread, bringing many blessings to the whole world and causing geniuses, saints and prophets to be born. Nothing is more important than this work. Without it man is a walking corpse. Understand what I am saying and you will leave here happy, because you will sense that your life has taken on unsuspected meaning.

One day, all the spiritual movements will become one with the Universal White Brotherhood — all because of that one essential element that is lacking to them and that we possess: brotherhood. For the last 2000 years, in spite of Christ's Teaching, nothing has been achieved for the good of the collectivity. Human beings continue to destroy and devour each other everywhere, even within their own families and their own societies, simply because they lack this element of love. With love, the Kingdom of God will become a reality. Events are beginning to move faster; our Teaching will soon spread throughout the world and it is essential that it should, because it is the one thing that is capable of awakening a new consciousness in human beings and showing them that, by working only for themselves, they have been on the wrong track for centuries. When that Golden Age comes, you will see the bliss, the splendour and the abundance enjoyed by human beings throughout the world: they will love each other, sing together and be full of admiration for each other.

If you have understood me; if you leave here determined to work for that collective life, you will find that you will be very happy to be living and working with others and very proud of yourself. You will become radiantly luminous, beautiful and expressive. It is better to be illiterate but happy in a life of fulfilment than to be learned and socially prominent but unhappy, worried and anxious. There is nothing worse than a high degree of intellectual education if it is not accompanied by a sound education of the heart. Intellectuals are self-satisfied and give themselves airs because they have acquired a mass of information, but they often lack kindness, humility, simplicity and generosity. The worth of an individual does not depend on how much he knows but on his kindness, light and love; for everything else can disappear, but these qualities will never disappear.

There was once a brilliant scholar who thought he would like to go for a sail, so he hired a fisherman to take him out to sea in his boat. As they were sailing along, the sky became more and more menacing but the scholar was too busy talking to the fisherman to notice. 'My good man', he was saying, 'Have you studied chemistry?' 'No, sir', replied the fisherman, 'My father was poor and I started to work when I was young'. 'What a pity,' said the scholar; 'A quarter of your life gone to waste. But, perhaps you know something about physics?' 'Not a thing, Your Excellency! My father and mother...' and the fisherman began his tale all over again. 'My poor man, two quarters of your life lost!' lamented the scholar; 'And astronomy? Astronomy is really wonderful... all about the constellations and the nebulae...' 'Never heard of it!' said the boatman. 'My family, etc., etc.' 'Poor

fellow', exclaimed his passenger, 'Three quarters of your life lost!'
The little boat went farther and farther out to sea, the storm
became more violent and the waves threatened to engulf them.
'Your Honour', cried the poor, ignorant fisherman, 'Do you know
how to swim?' 'No, I don't.' replied the scholar. 'Well, Sir,' was
the reply, 'That's four quarters of your life gone for ever!'

Well here, in the Brotherhood, you are learning to swim in the
ocean of life. You must start, now, to improve every aspect of
your life, to renew and resuscitate everything, to turn your face in
the direction of immensity and dedicate yourself to the work of the
collectivity. And don't tell me that you have a family and children
who prevent you from devoting yourself to this work. It is precisely this idea of brotherhood that will help you to bring up your
children properly: they will admire and defend you because you
will be a model for them to follow. Children often cause their
parents great unhappiness because they blame them for having
brought them up, without realizing it, in a very narrow mentality,
for not having opened them to perspectives of nobleness and light.
Parents are often too intent on improving the material conditions
of their children; they neglect their spirit and then their spirit feels
stifled and rebels. I am not saying that parents must bear all the
blame. No, but much of the responsibility is theirs.

Change your point of view, therefore; dedicate yourselves
to the work of the collectivity and every aspect of your lives
will fall into place. Human beings need spiritual nourishment
and they will end by abandoning you if you are incapable of
giving them what they need. Work for the collectivity, therefore,
and be bolder about promoting our ideas. The attitude towards
spirituality is improving remarkably in the world, today; you
must not keep all these treasures for yourselves: spread the light
of this Teaching to those around you. A lot of people in the
world are suffering; they have been thrown off balance and are
looking for answers. Why not help them? Go ahead; don't just
stand there like stones; broadcast love and light and all the
treasures of our Teaching all around you.

A few minutes of silent meditation.

In the silence I could feel that many friends from the invisible world were here to watch over you. Yes, many invisible friends came to help you and relieve you of some of your burdens. This is why I stopped talking: to leave them free to do their work. And when you go home they will still be with you, they will continue to work in you, for they need workers. Believe me, if you refuse to work with them for the triumph of light in the world, you will be bringing suffering on yourself, for they will deprive you of many blessings. You must constantly focus on this one idea: the Kingdom of God on earth. Even if you don't succeed in establishing it outwardly, it will, at least, be established within you and that is already something. For no effort ever goes unrewarded; it always produces a result of some kind. Even if you fail to convert the whole of humanity − in any case, some people are so intractable that any such success is out of the question − you yourself will be better off.

Personally, I believe that the Kingdom of God will come. Exactly how is not yet clear, but one thing is sure: before the end of the century it will be there. And this means that there must be workers, workers who are disinterested and unafraid: unafraid to commit themselves, to be ridiculed or to die of hunger, and who understand that they must use everything as a means to attain this Heavenly goal. All that we possess in the way of faculties, talents or material advantages must be employed in the service of a divine ideal. And not just the opposite, as is often the case today. People put their gifts and talents at the service of their belly, their sexual appetites, their vanity or their thirst for power. They behave as though Heaven itself were there to serve their every whim. Believe me: the Angels and Archangels and the Lord Himself are there for no other purpose. Does that astonish you? I assure you, it's the truth; without realizing it, human beings do this all the time: they put their best and most beautiful qualities at the service of their egoism.

There, these few explanations should help you to have clearer notions about certain things. Let me recapitulate: we must leave a lot of space in our lives for Cosmic Intelligence, so that it may come to us, so that It may dwell in us and do Its work in us. Cosmic Intelligence is ceaselessly at work in us, sending us rays and particles which come to us from space and really want to impregnate us so as to help us to grow and improve. The reason why human beings are not improving is that, in fact, they do everything possible to prevent Cosmic Intelligence from entering them and helping them. By giving way to their weaknesses and vices, they surround themselves with a shell that makes them impervious to Its influence. Sacrifice and self-renunciation are the only things that can strip away this shell. Every time you renounce a vice or a bad habit you are opening a door to the world of light.

Since so many friends from the invisible world are willing to help you and make you free, why must you continually put obstacles in their way? Open your hearts and souls to them. Welcome them. Tell them that you need them: 'Oh, great spirits of light, I need you. Enter me and purify me, give me your light!' Open yourselves; let Heaven flood into you and, little by little, the Kingdom of God will be established on earth.

The Bonfin, October 1, 1972

Chapter Three

Youth and Revolution

I*

Nowadays, young people spend years studying and reading in college or at the University and this, in itself, is excellent. The only trouble is that this single-minded concentration on intellectual formation is actually a hindrance to true education. They don't develop character or learn how to behave: they are morally adrift. Intellectual knowledge can never touch the depths of the human soul, it will always be something superficial — and as soon as their exams are over, don't all students hasten to forget everything they have learned? In any case, most of them only study in order to get a diploma which will open the door to opportunity, power or prestige: that is what they are really after. They are in no way transformed by what they learn.

And yet, the thing that should most concern youth is transformation. That is what we offer them here, in the Teaching: methods and exercises and all the elements they need to transform themselves, for no amount of intellectual information can achieve this: other elements are needed. You can study all the

* The five short lectures included in this chapter were given at the time of the student uprising in France, in May 1968. See also *Complete Works*, vol. 12, chapters 1 to 7.

sacred Scriptures, all the Bibles and Korans that have ever been printed, but nothing will change unless you add that other, inner element. Transformation is a process that one can only do oneself, by one's own active participation, one's own desire, one's own will-power and decision. These are the inner forces that have the power to awaken the qualities and virtues that have lain dormant within us since the Lord created us at the beginning of time.

Today, everybody, even the most primitive peoples, have the opportunity to go to school. No doubt this is a good thing, but one cannot help but see that unrest and revolt are still rampant. In fact, revolt seems to be a by-product of education. Why do learning and intellectual development — which are, after all, excellent in themselves — so often give rise to war and disaster? Actually, it is not knowledge as such that is at fault but the nature of that knowledge. The first thing people see, when their eyes are opened, is social injustice: they see that others are rich and powerful while they are poor and powerless. Naturally, their jealousy and anger are aroused and they begin to hanker for all kinds of things that they never wanted before, and then, as they see no other way of getting them, they take the simplest approach, which is that of violence. This is how education so often ends by arousing every form of greed. Now, don't jump to the conclusion that I think people should be left in illiteracy and ignorance. Not at all! I am not in favour of ignorance, but nor am I in favour of the kind of knowledge that only serves to arouse men's lower nature.

But let's forget about the education of primitive peoples for the moment, and focus on the situation in what we call the civilized world. What are we seeing here, more and more? On the pretext of intellectual sophistication, the majority is being lured ever deeper into the morass. They have no notion of the structure of human beings and think that they have every right and can do whatever they please. And, indeed, they can do whatever they please — until what they do ends by unleashing such powerful negative forces within themselves that they find themselves trapped and doomed with no hope of escape. They plunge recklessly into danger saying, with a clear conscience, that it is in these depths that they experience the powerful sensations they enjoy, that they find ecstasy in destruction and disaster. This is how they present the situation: as a deliberate choice of degradation. It is an entirely new current of madness that is creeping into human beings today. One wonders whether some of these people should not be put under medical observation.

Even more serious is the fact that they influence others and, as neither the authorities nor the Law do anything to prevent it, they are free to be as destructive as they please and to lead thousands to their doom. But, good Heavens! One should never launch into experiences of this kind with such a serene disregard for the dangers involved. There are circumstances in which a certain dose of fear is good and necessary. But no! They are unafraid; with their eyes wide open they march straight towards the precipice. This is the greatest danger facing mankind today. War and disease are less to be feared than this wrong-headed philosophy, for it is more capable than any plague, famine or war of destroying mankind.

Of course, I know very well that young people will reject my point of view outright. In fact, they will probably label me as 'bourgeois' (I must say that I have never understood exactly what a 'bourgeois' is supposed to be nor why it is considered so reprehensible. Perhaps someone could enlighten me?) As I was saying, young people will not admit that my philosophy is based on a knowledge of the universe and on the laws which govern both the universe and man. You are not entitled to talk at random, to say whatever comes into your head in the conviction that everything is true, that there is room in the world for every idea, however far-fetched. It is just not so! You are not at liberty to try everything, to do whatever you fancy, for every act or gesture necessarily leads to specific consequences.

Man is not separate from nature; we are part of nature; we live and breathe in nature; our relation with nature is reciprocal for, just as nature influences us, so do we influence nature. This is why we are not free to do whatever our fancy dictates. We must be considerate and in control of ourselves and live in loving communion with this great Whole instead of always trying to dominate it or exploit it for our own benefit. The sun, the stars and the planets all move in accordance with the laws of Cosmic Intelligence; only man thinks he has the right to go against the order, balance and harmony of the Whole. He refuses, even, to admit that the Whole surpasses him in intelligence. Oh no! Man is the prince, the lord of all, and the world is there for his pleasure.

You only have to look at modern paintings in which everything is contrary to nature. They call it 'abstract'. Very well, I have no objection to abstractions, but is it really necessary to represent human beings and landscapes 'abstractly', with bizarre, unrecognizable lines and forms that evoke nothing so much as the chaos from which human beings emerged? Doesn't life offer enough examples of how things should be? Suppose you are starting to build a house: the building site is strewn with untidy piles of steel and timber, bricks, cement and sand. Little by little, first the foundations and then the walls emerge and, eventually, all that disorder has disappeared and we see a house with freshly painted shutters, bright new curtains and window boxes full of flowers. In the beginning all was chaos and in the end it is a finished, aesthetic work of art. Or suppose you are cooking a meal: the raw ingredients on your kitchen table don't look very appetizing but, when you finally take the piping hot dish out of the oven and garnish it before setting it before your guests... Mmm! How good it looks and smells! And take the example of man himself: to begin with he is nothing more than a minute drop of liquid, and then, little by little, he begins to take shape and, one fine day, a beautiful baby is born.

This is the natural process that can be seen throughout the universe: out of chaos comes order, beauty and perfection. But, today, we are witnessing the exact opposite, especially in the arts: human beings are reverting to chaos. You look at a painting and wonder whether it is supposed to represent a human being, a horse or a ship. There is no longer any differentiation. But the intelligence of nature works in exactly the opposite direction: it emphasizes differentiation. A single cell divides and, within a few months, becomes a richly complex human being. And should we now reverse the process and go back to being unicellular? No, that would be a retrogression, a degeneration, and it is precisely towards this degeneration that some ignorant, unenlightened artists want to lead us, whereas our true goal must always be the perfect accomplishment, the final consummation of a work.

Nature doesn't stop working on what she has begun until it is a finished product and, one day, she will finish and perfect man, just as she perfects animals, flowers and crystals. But, in the meantime, our 'pontiffs' of poetry, painting and music are edging us ever closer to chaos, with words strung aimlessly together so that everybody finds whatever meaning he chooses in them, or with bizarre sounds that pass as music or, in painting and sculpture, with their asymmetrical figures with exaggeratedly elongated or swollen limbs. And all this is bad magic, for the men and women who read or look or listen to these 'works of art' are carried back to the furthest, darkest days of the earth.

The Book of Genesis says, 'In the beginning God created the heavens and the earth. The earth was without form, and void; and darkness was upon the face of the deep. And the Spirit of God was hovering over the face of the waters.' And the point is this: if the Spirit of God moved over the face of the waters, it was in order to organize the world. And if we have emerged from chaos it is not in order to sink back into it again. Is this quite clear to you? This being the case, why, instead of giving a place of honour to artists who would bring about the Kingdom of God, do people reward those who degrade and defile humanity with such resounding success? Write a really indecent book and it will sell millions of copies and be translated into all the languages in the world. But write something that makes really good sense and you won't get two people to read it, because the entire world is caught up in the folly of wanting to try everything, to experience everything: this madness is spreading like a prairie fire!

Well, whatever anybody else does, I shall continue to live according to my own philosophy — for my own sake, first of all — and leave others to experiment with all the systems and theories they wish. But they must be warned that all this can only end in disaster for, if these conditions prevail and there are no more rules or laws, there will be no more society. This is why it pains me to see all that is going on. It is no longer a question of a few isolated individuals who have lost their heads; it has become a collective phenomenon on a vast scale. How can it be prevented from spreading even further? No one is willing to come and help us. No one cares. But I care; it concerns me deeply, for the fate of the world is my one great concern. I care about nothing else, I think of nothing else, night and day: the fate of the world and how to help it to achieve its destiny.

I am very much aware that young people are being thrown seriously off balance by their studies... worse: they are being spiritually annihilated and, for this reason, they are less at fault than people say. Adults have given them a very bad example. The young are victims of the culture in which they are brought up: the films they see, the books and magazines they read, the conversations and speeches they listen to. They are formed, fashioned and impregnated by the questionable theories expounded by artists, writers and politicians who have no sense of responsibility. All those people are adults and yet it seems that they have never paused to reflect that the spoken or written word or the images on a screen have the power to ruin the mental health of their audience. If the young have no respect for anyone any more, it is the fault of those who teach them and bring them up. They have failed in their task and the only thing left to them is to recognize that these young people they are so ready to condemn are no more than a faithful reflection of themselves and, instead of being so sure of themselves, to acknowledge that it is they who have made them what they are. Let them draw a lesson from this and decide to change.

Don't think that this means that I approve of young people unreservedly. Adults and young alike are all in need of light; they all need to study Initiatic Science. Young people have no right to show disrespect for their elders. What do they know about life? Have they shown themselves exceptional in any way? Are they capable of doing any better than their parents? As long as they still have things to learn, as long as they have not proved themselves, they must behave with respect and continue to study. Only when they have passed their exams and are capable of shouldering heavy responsibilities will they have the right to change things as much as they like.

One day, when Paganini was giving a concert in Naples, with the hall filled to capacity and everyone applauding his prodigious talent, he noticed a young man in the audience who was not clapping and sat staring at him with a sneer on his face. This angered Paganini so much that, amidst all the uproar of applause and curtain calls, he announced that he would not come back to take a bow until the boy had been brought to him. This was done and Paganini said to him, 'I would like to know, young man, not only why you did not applaud but also why you have that mocking smile on your lips. I don't like it. Explain yourself!' 'Oh, Maestro', said the boy, 'There is no one on earth who appreciates you as much as I do. My smile comes from resentment and grief because, you see, I'm a composer and, until this evening, I thought I was a great musician... and now I know I'm not. For me, it's all over! Now that I've heard you I can only be desperately disillusioned with myself.' 'What is your name?' asked Paganini. 'Vicenzo Bellini', replied the young man. Disarmed, Paganini immediately began to encourage him and helped him to become one of the world's great composers.

Isn't that an interesting story?

The Bonfin, July 6, 1968

II

I don't blame young people for taking the wrong road; I simply say that they are imbibing ideas and examples which are far from magnificent. We should not try to destroy all the old traditions; there's a great deal of good in traditions which are the outcome of thousands of years of experience. Men have spent their lives searching and suffering and groping their way and, thanks to their efforts, have discovered a certain number of rules on which they have built their culture and civilization. Some of these forms need to be changed; that is true. But that does not mean that everything must be thrown overboard, especially when no one has any idea how to replace what exists with something better. Do I go around destroying traditions? Certainly not! I am in favour of tradition on condition that it be adapted to our own times. But young people, who have no proper perception of present-day reality nor of what it should be, simply follow their impulses and rush into action blindly, changing this and destroying that without a thought for the consequences.

Let's take it, then, that young people want a revolution. They want to upset the existing order. But have they ever asked themselves whether they have the right to overturn anything and everything? Whether there are not certain immutable laws which no creature has the right to transgress? Life has its laws, laws that are studied by chemists, physicists, biologists, etc. and, whether we like it or not, we cannot go against those laws without being destroyed by them. Believe me, there are such things as immutable principles and anyone who tries to deny them is condemning himself to darkness and death. Of course, I know that young people justify themselves by saying that they are dissatisfied with what adults offer them. This I understand, for I am equally dissatisfied! But I still cannot side with them, for the freedom they are demanding, the freedom to do whatever they please, is not at all ideal or divine.

Freedom! Liberty! Well, however much you repeat the slogan, 'Liberty, Equality, Fraternity!' there is really no liberty and no equality; of the three, only fraternity exists. I assure you: there is no such thing as liberty, freedom. How can you talk of man being free when he is a slave to his own appetites and pleasures, his family, his physical circumstances and the constraints of time? God alone is free and man will be free only when he identifies with God, when he becomes one with God. Outside of God there is no such thing as liberty. Licence? Yes, there's plenty of that and, for many, this is what the notion of liberty has become: a total lack of respect for everyone and everything. But the danger of this is that others can do the same; you will not be the only one who thinks he has the right to be unjust and violent; others will retaliate in kind. But nobody bargains for that. You are in love with violence? Well, I can understand that. I may have a tendency in that direction myself − wouldn't I just love to set the whole world on fire! − but that is not sufficient reason for doing so.

Human beings think they have the right to be violent, and then they are pained and surprised when others react in the same way. You must realize that every act or gesture on your part triggers a similar act on the part of others. Be generous with someone and they will be generous with you. Something in them will whisper, 'Ah, I'll just show you how kind, noble and generous I can be, too!' and then it becomes a battle of smiles and gifts; a battle of love. This is what is so wonderful, and it is something that people have never really understood: the law of echo, of rebound. They say, 'Just let me get my hands on that fellow: I'll break his jaw!' And I say, 'Go ahead! Hit him... you'll see where that gets you!' But they are astonished when they get some of their own medicine in return. Young people think that they are justified in doing what they please to others but they object when others do the same to them. But you must never forget that this law exists and that it makes others reflect your own behaviour. They cannot do otherwise: if you start something they are obliged to retaliate.

If you think that everyone is going to let you ride roughshod over them without hitting back, you are very much mistaken. Sooner or later the law will strike back. If you have no respect for anyone, no one will have any respect for you. You need not expect to receive respect if you never give it. If you want others to respect you, you have to begin by respecting them. If there is one law I have proved to my satisfaction, it is this one. All my life I have shown respect for others and now I can see the law at work: others respect me. Sometimes, in fact, I wonder why. It is because, having spent my whole life respecting others, I have triggered a movement which is now bouncing back to me.

The young feel free to break laws because they think that they are merely rules devised by adults. No; very often, behind the laws of men, are the laws of nature. Take the rules about sexuality, for instance: young people think that they are hopelessly old-fashioned and obsolete − 'bourgeois' and 'reactionary' as they say − and they want to do away with them and give a free rein to their instincts and passions. They have no notion of the consequences this would lead to in every area. In the area of health alone: don't they know that whole nations have been wiped out before now by venereal disease? And it's no good thinking that recent medical advances, antibiotics and so on, will protect them. When a nation loses all self-control and allows everyone to give a free rein to his passions and sexual appetites, it is signing its own death warrant. Mankind has had, after all, many thousands of years of experience and that is not to be despised. If young people think that the laws are there to protect the rich and oppress them, they are wrong. Human beings have learned, in the course of the last few thousand years, that they cannot live together in society without a certain number of rules; that no culture or civilization can survive if it is not based on law. Without law, society is a jungle. Of course, some people get round the law or make it serve their own ends, but that is not a reason for demolishing everything.

When the young abandon themselves to excesses of disorder and licentiousness, they are like children gobbling up pots of jam when their parents' back is turned. They will only make themselves sick! The Sages understood all that a long time ago; this is why they laid down certain rules of abstinence, self-control and prudence. Recently, in France, there were all kinds of slogans painted on the walls encouraging people to kick over the traces: 'Live without law', 'Orgasm unlimited', 'Love ad lib', 'Disobey', etc. But this is the world standing on its head! It is all very well for students to discuss and argue and vociferate and make demands, but they have no idea of what the long-term consequences would be if their demands were met. They never think about how one thing leads to another. In fact, only the Initiates have ever really looked at the problem of the long-term effects of thoughts, words and gestures.

If young people had more discernment, if they realized that, when they refuse to obey the rules, they are undermining their own strength by releasing the powers of darkness within themselves, perhaps they would not be in such a hurry to clamour for all these liberties. The law is absolute: the less you control your thoughts, desires and appetites the more you will be enslaved. You say that you must satisfy every passing whim. Well, do so if you really want to but that is the best way to become a slave – a slave to yourself or, rather, to the primitive forces within you, for they will overpower you and keep you completely under their thumb. You can never be king of your own kingdom until you learn self-control; weakness, ill-health and even madness will always be lying in wait for you. If this were not so, the Sages of all ages would have advised us to satisfy all our cravings. If they have never done so it is because they know that this is the quickest route to Hell and destruction.

But, nowadays, destruction is all the rage! In the universities, doors were torn off their hinges and statues smashed. Destruction is becoming more and more popular: young people enjoy destroying things. Even here, a few days ago, some vandals came and tore up all the flowers from the Rock[1]. Is this how parents bring up their children today? Children must be taught to respect everything — living creatures, plants and even inanimate objects — not to destroy them. Perhaps you will say, 'Oh, it was only a few flowers!' I know, but if you begin by uprooting flowers, you'll end by uprooting hearts and souls and consciences and everything divine.

It is perfectly true that we are living in a society in which a great many things need to be changed, but this must not be achieved by violence. In any case, violence never brings about true change; it only makes things worse. How, then, can we transform society? By our own way of life. If we begin by changing ourselves we shall end by changing the whole world. This is why, in the Brotherhood, we are working to become a tangible example of a better kind of society. We are endeavouring to become a solid core of highly conscious, resolute men and women who will prove that mankind is capable of becoming one family, one brotherhood. Our first task, therefore, is to transform ourselves into living examples and even, one could say, to impose this example on others, not by physical force, of course, but by the nobility, magnanimity, light and spiritual beauty emanating from us.

---

1 The Rock is a rocky platform at the top of a hill near the Bonfin where the Master and his disciples gather every morning, in spring and summer, to meditate and watch the sun rise.

The need to feel their own strength and power drives too many young people to reckless actions. They don't realize that true strength is inner strength, the ability to control and master themselves, to show themselves to be noble, great-hearted, perfect. Initiates, too, want to become strong and powerful but they know what true greatness and true power are, whereas so many young people, by giving way to their instincts and seeking power through violence and destruction, merely weaken themselves and become the slaves of their own base instincts and vices.

Believe me, my dear brothers and sisters, I am completely impartial: I love all these young people and I love their elders, but I believe that both are at fault: the adults because they have not known how to educate the young and, especially, how to give them a good example, and the young, because they think they can settle all their problems through revolution and violence and by destroying everything that adults have done. I advise both the young and adults to come and be enlightened here, in the Universal White Brotherhood, for it alone possesses a philosophy capable of solving all the problems of mankind, be they economic, social, political − or even military.

The Bonfin, July 10, 1968

III

What about all those black flags that we used to see everywhere? In my ignorance I didn't even know what a black flag stood for, so I asked some friends and was told that it stood for anarchy. Anarchy? Is that something good? Something you can eat or drink? Will someone please explain? You'll be thinking, 'Good Lord, what ignorance! He doesn't even know what anarchy is.' Actually, what is far more important is that I don't know how people are going to survive when everything is disorganized and destroyed, when there are no more laws, institutions or government. I can see that the pleasure of destroying everything may make you happy for a little while, it may make you feel very cock-a-hoop, drunk with power, but still, you also have to think about what life will be like once you've destroyed everything. Is it possible to envisage a world in which there are no governments, no police or magistrates? Yes, it is, but only if human beings are perfect. In that case, as everybody would spontaneously behave so rationally and with such virtue, neither rules nor regulations nor punitive measures would be necessary. However, as human beings are still very far from this state of perfection, society must still be organized and regulated.

As I say, there's no doubt that the present state of society is far from perfect, but it is the fruit of thousands and thousands of years of painful experience and it is certainly better than at many other periods of history. For a long time to come men will still have to search and grope and change first this and then that, until they eventually find the ideal government for an ideal society. It would be impossible to enumerate all the philosophers who have thought and written about this question − from Plato, in the *Republic*, down to the present day. But, so far, no one has ever achieved the ideal society and the world continues to muddle along as best it can on the basis of past acquisitions, some of which are sound and others less so. And that is why, today, there is so much unrest and people want to turn everything upside down. As you very well know, I too want things to change, but any changes that are made must improve conditions for all creatures and that, I fear, is still not the case. If some people really think that things can be put right simply by provoking explosions and volcanic eruptions, they must be extremely stupid. I certainly wouldn't advise any friend of mine to vote for or lend a hand to anarchists who have no more intelligence than that. Leave them to their own resources: they'll come to a sticky end without any help from you.

I readily admit that there are a few real revolutionaries such as Lenin, Mao Tse-tung and Fidel Castro. But people like that didn't destroy everything. Besides, can you say that things are really better since their revolutions? No; nothing is really different except, perhaps, that the man at the top has disappeared and someone else has taken his place. The rhetoric has changed a little, the slogans are not the same, the songs are new, but the vice and crime, the fear and corruption are still the same.

Anarchists are incapable of doing anything constructive. Some revolutionaries can be constructive, perhaps, if they are very intelligent and generous and work to improve the situation rather than making it even more intolerable. History shows that tyrants come and go: they may rise to power and liquidate their enemies, but they cannot stay on top for long. For this, too, is a law of life: a tyrant, by his very tyranny, attracts others of the same kind who end by destroying him. You know the saying: 'They sow the wind, and reap the whirlwind'.

If these young people, these so-called revolutionaries were capable of seeing what goes on inside them, they would realize that, when they indulge in wild, unprincipled behaviour, their whole organism is impregnated by the violent, chaotic vibrations they stir up and that their contempt and lack of respect for others will be forever etched into their cells. But they don't try to see into themselves and they don't know that Nature – who is not only intelligent but who never forgets anything – has a lesson or two in store for them. Perhaps they will marry and have children who will be exactly like them, and then it will be their turn to suffer violence and a lack of respect. And they won't enjoy that at all... but it will be no more than justice!

The young have chosen anarchy? Very well; let them have it, but the laws are merciless: anarchy will take control of their beings and, later on in life, they will be subjected to identical reactions from their own children or the people around them. Then they will start moaning about injustice and declaring that they have done nothing to deserve such dreadful children. Not deserve them, indeed! Have they forgotten how they behaved when they were young? Let them remember that and then they will begin to understand. But it will be too late. The damage will have been done. The boomerang effect exists in the psychic as well as in the physical world, but it is only when the consequences of their acts rebound and hit them on the head that people begin to reflect.

If I had to give you a really exceptional example I would not choose any of the great Initiates of the past, but someone you all know: Socrates. After he had been condemned to death, some of his disciples tried to persuade him to let them organize his escape but he refused to leave his prison, saying that a good citizen should obey the laws of his city. One cannot help but refer constantly to the example of this great man who, although he never wrote anything, has continued to influence men's minds for the last twenty-four centuries. Of course, this is largely thanks to Plato, who was his disciple, and Plato and his own disciple, Aristotle, are still the twin peaks of philosophy; no philosopher since has ever surpassed them. But what an extraordinary man Socrates was! He had the face of a satyr and, in fact, he confessed that this was because he had, once, been very vicious, but that he had succeeded in conquering his vices; it was a thing of the past. So his merit was all the greater.

I am sure you all know the story of Socrates' life: how he married Xanthippe (whom I have often mentioned) and how he strolled through the streets and public places of Athens, teaching his fellow citizens simply by talking to them and asking them awkward questions. Although he was very popular with the people, his integrity and outspokenness gained him some powerful enemies and, in a plot to get rid of him, they arrested him on trumped-up charges of corrupting the youth of Athens and he was condemned to drink the cup of hemlock. Socrates could certainly have escaped death if he had wanted to, but he refused and it was precisely because he was conscious of his innocence that he was able to accept his sentence so fearlessly. What calmness and courage he demonstrated in his last moments! You have probably read the account of his farewell to the gaoler who told him that the time had come for him to drink the poison, of how he asked the man who brought him the cup exactly what he should do and how he followed his instructions to the letter. Then there was that encounter with his disciples shortly before he died... After all these centuries, the death of Socrates still lives as something unique in the memory of men.

You may say, 'Surely, he must have had special guidance?' Yes, of course. All the sages are guided. How could the Invisible World abandon a sage who possesses truth and respects the laws of God? Socrates was constantly accompanied by an entity which he called his *daemon* (the meaning of this term in Greek has nothing to do with the Christian notion of the Devil or of Hell).

Socrates' *daemon* was a very exalted spirit who guided and coun-
selled him. All sages have one — sometimes several — of these
guides.

If young people would only accept to learn, they would discover within themselves all the same truths and laws that the sages
have discovered over the ages by observing what went on in nature
and comparing it with what they saw happening in themselves.
All sages come to the conclusion that life is based on laws of harmony, disinterestedness and love and that, if one fails to respect
these laws, everything falls apart. This is how moral laws were
discovered. And what I find especially inspiring in Socrates is that
he understood that what matters most is the way you live. In this
he was very different from other philosophers and sophists of
his day who claimed to know all that physics and metaphysics
had to teach and be able to discourse about everything. Socrates
concentrated on the study of man; he adopted as his personal
motto the famous inscription from the temple of Delphi, 'Know
thyself.' All true Masters have the same philosophy. What is good
and true for one is good and true for them all; they all teach the
same ethic, the same philosophical system. Depending on time
and place, there will be some minor differences, but the funda-
mental principles are always identical.

Initiates refuse to have anything to do with anarchy because
they know only too well that they would be the first to be affected by the ensuing illness, disorder and destruction; that anarchy
would destroy them. As soon as you open your heart to the seeds
of dissolution, invisible currents and forces begin to ravage your
whole being. It won't happen all at once, of course; but, little
by little, you will disintegrate. Even physical health depends on
obedience to this universal order — call it what you will: synarchy,
hierarchy or divine monarchy — and, once a man begins to establish that order within himself, every part of him finds its balance
and he dwells in peace, harmony and beauty. He is illuminated
and strengthened; he receives new life and begins to vibrate in
unison with the whole cosmos, with the Heavenly regions above.

He becomes a gushing spring, an ever-flowing source of light; radiance streams from him. This is the higher man, the ideal man that we are all meant to be, instead of being a door flung wide to every destructive current that swirls round us in the form of anarchistic philosophies and ideologies. All those, be they individuals, families, social groups or whole countries... all who open themselves to these currents destroy themselves. The law is absolute and it is essential to give it an important place in one's life.

Blessed are they who understand this! They have the power to trigger unlimited forces within their own being and then to see how these eternal forces work within them to liberate and transform them. And those harum-scarum bunches of young rebels with their black flags must realize that they will not succeed in destroying society. Society needs to be improved and it will be, but only by good example, work and selflessness. Sooner or later, in the presence of these qualities, things are bound to change. The attempt to change things in any other way can only justify those who say, 'The more things change, the more the filth is the same'! Without light there will never be any real change. There is no need to invent new systems, revolutionary or otherwise. Nothing needs to be invented, all the solutions we need have already been invented by Nature. All we have to do is rediscover them.

The Bonfin, July 16, 1968

IV

The young are eager for revolution, they want to jettison all our traditions and, in order to demonstrate the lengths to which they are prepared to go, they apparently marched to the *Arc de Triomphe* and threw excrement on the tomb of the Unknown Soldier. This just shows how little they value the sacrifice of men to whom we owe life and liberty. When one thinks of all those who have worked and struggled for the Charter of Human Rights, who fought and laid down their lives so that men might live in freedom and mutual respect... and now they want to destroy all that. I cannot believe that anyone can seriously approve or encourage this kind of behaviour. It is true that the young are capable of changing the world, but only on condition that they show true superiority: superiority of behaviour, superiority of language and superiority of intelligence. There are better ways of changing the world than by defiling the tomb of an unknown soldier who poured out his lifeblood so that France might be free. How can anyone not understand and appreciate this?

If young people were working to make human beings truly great, to fulfil the needs of their divine nature − instead of pandering only to their baser appetites, as everyone has been doing for thousands of years − they would be acclaimed today as the new prophets and the world would be at the dawn of a new life, a new civilization. But, as they are not sufficiently enlightened and their ideal is far too prosaic, they are betraying their mission. If there is any fun to be had they come running, but they are not interested in making the slightest effort. I see no ideal of human dignity or perfection there; in fact, their conduct is worse than that of the average man and woman. Most people, after all, make some attempt to control themselves and obey some rules; they often blunder, of course, but they regret their faults and try to make amends and improve. But for these young people there is no question of either amends or restraint. They are determined to experience the whole gamut of vice and disorder.

When someone has a sublime ideal it shows. He cannot help but express it in his language, in his attitudes and in the things he asks for. But what ideal is there, here? Are these young people working for the good of their country? Certainly not; if they were working for the good of France they would never have forced such a situation upon her. The truth is that they are working for the satisfaction of their baser needs. Millions of Frenchmen have made the supreme sacrifice so that their country might be great, wealthy and internationally respected and, now these young hooligans come along and hold it up to the world as an object of ridicule.

And what insolence in all that they do and say! If they had shown some sign of moral superiority when they presented their case to the University administrators and faculty, to the ministers, police and journalists, their demands would immediately have been taken seriously. But no; they simply insulted them and behaved as though they thought their attitude was exemplary. And yet, if others behaved in the same way to them, they would be furious; no one else has the right to be so insolent and vulgar. They are not even logical: if you give others an example, you have to expect them to follow it. If you are rude to them, they will be rude to you and there's no point in complaining about it. You can treat others as you please, but remember that they will treat you in exactly the same way; that is only logical and

just. Indeed, it is this total absence of logic that alarms me. How
can they believe that they will achieve their goals by behaving so
badly? Do they imagine that in spite of the violence and ugliness
of their conduct they will succeed? Not for a moment has it occurred to them that people will be disgusted and fed up with them.
In fact, it has come as quite a shock to them that they were not
being applauded from all sides.

Poor, ignorant youth! To be sure, it is only natural for young
people to be full of energy and enthusiasm, to feel the need to
express themselves, but have they ever paused to reflect on the
nature of the forces manifesting themselves in them, on where
they come from and whether they should obey all their dictates?
No, they never ask themselves such questions. They only know
that something inside them demands to be expressed. The truth
is that these young imbeciles who are making such a to-do and
demanding so much don't really know what they are doing. They
need to be enlightened, that's all. One day they will realize that
there are other ways of doing things and that they were on the
wrong track. How do they think they are going to change society?
By cutting down trees, tearing up paving stones or burning cars
and breaking windows? Is it intelligent to go about it by causing
vast amounts of damage? They are quite capable of setting fire
to Paris and then, like Nero, rejoicing and playing their fiddles
while they watch it burn! Believe me, the situation is very serious.

I cannot say that I am proud of the youth of the country.
Even if they are justified in their demands, there are other ways
of asking. 'Yes, but their professors refused to listen to them!'
I still maintain that there are other ways of making oneself heard:
by high-mindedness and intelligence, for instance. If they showed
these qualities, everyone would listen to them, but they won't
listen to them if they start burning and destroying everything.
Besides, even if they were given everything they asked for, they
would still not be satisfied because what they are asking for is
the gratification of all their baser needs − and the gratification
of those needs can never truly satisfy a human being. If they were

given the sexual freedom they demand, for instance, would they be any happier? Would it give them health and peace of mind? On the contrary, it would destroy their mental balance and make them fit candidates for a mental asylum. No, no! They can't convince me. The things they are demanding and the way they are going about it leave me entirely unconvinced. They may convince a great many idiots, but they fail to convince me.

It is by no means certain, for instance, that the changes they are demanding in the curriculum would be an improvement. Some things certainly need to be changed, but are the young always capable of distinguishing the good from the bad in their curriculum? All they want is to eliminate the things they don't like or which seem too difficult. I would be very interested to know exactly what they do propose to keep and what they would get rid of. If they are going to make demands, it is important that they should understand why they demand this or that. As to those who are going to have to respond to the students' demands, they have no clear idea, either, as to what they should refuse and what they should accept. In cases like this, instead of being guided by higher principles, they are almost always guided by any ideas that happen to be in fashion and, in this way, their attempts to solve the immediate problem only create other, long term problems. You have to look well ahead if you want to avoid unwise decisions that will make things worse.

I am aware, of course, that many young men and girls in the Brotherhood have become involved in these upheavals. They feel obliged to stick together and express their solidarity with their comrades — even when their actions are outrageous. But let me tell them that they must never endorse violence and hooliganism. There are laws by which we are responsible for what we do and, in the long run, they will be punished by the Invisible World for condoning these senseless acts. They must not do it; they should not have got themselves involved; our Teaching is above these conflicts. But these young brothers and sisters plunged into the

mêlée, forgetting that, when one allows oneself to be carried away
by currents that are not pure one cannot help but be tainted by
impurity oneself. All those who have had any part in these disturbances have been soiled by them and it is up to me, now, to wash
them and get them clean again because they have picked up a
lot of very bad particles. They don't realize it, of course, because
they cannot discern these things yet; but I can see their condition
very clearly.

If the young people in the Brotherhood are going to be exactly
like all those frenetic youngsters who are agitating for change,
what is the use of the Teaching? The mentality in the Brotherhood should be quite different from the general mentality; we
should be a good example and prove ourselves by behaving according to a totally different logic. How can the Brotherhood
prove that it has found the light if its members don't prepare themselves for their role? It is sad to see that, when there are disturbances of this kind, even very minor ones, our brothers and
sisters behave as though they had never learned or understood
anything different. You should be above disorders of this kind
and try to communicate some light, try to help and advise others
and pour oil on troubled waters and, if they refuse to listen, you
must let them go their own way and take the consequences. But
to aid and abet unruliness and revolt is a grave fault and you will
be held responsible for having encouraged the forces of evil
instead of the forces of good.

It is not that I have an axe to grind one way or the other.
I am above all this agitation and I would have liked the members
of the Brotherhood to be above it also. But, what can you expect?
They have not yet reached that level and several threw themselves
into the fray on one side or the other. When are my brothers
and sisters going to understand that they must not behave like
that? That they must be an example for others and that, whatever happens in the political arena, they must stay above the turmoil and exercise a calming influence? I can understand that
others do such foolish things... but not the brothers and sisters!

They possess enough light and experience to know that they must not get drawn into the mêlée.

To be sure, complete neutrality doesn't really exist. In one way or another we are obliged to have a part in everything that happens in the world. This is true for me, too: even if I take no active part in political events, because it is not my role to do so, inwardly I cannot avoid participating in what is happening. I don't recommend that the brothers and sisters join in the demonstrations and march through the streets shouting and gesticulating, but I was still very glad to hear (I was out of the country when all this was going on), that there had been a huge rally in the *Champs-Elysées* to show support for the President. That doesn't contradict what I have been saying. One cannot help but be affected by events. I cannot help but give my support to all the good I see in the world; my spirit takes part in it all without my saying a word. I am always eager to send a few particles of my being to support a divine cause. Even if I don't come forward and start making speeches, in my soul, in my thoughts and my innermost being, it is as though I were physically present: I vote, I talk to people and try to explain things to them. My whole being is called into action. If I tell you not to get involved in the turmoil it is because the cause is almost never divine; if the cause were divine I would never reproach anyone for getting involved.

Yes, we have to win through; we have to be strong enough to triumph over difficulties, but Initiatic Science has never taught that strength consists in destroying and plundering. On the contrary, Initiatic Science teaches that true strength consists in remaining at the centre, in that central core of light and warmth, of intelligence and love. For my part, all my life I have endeavoured to come closer to this centre so as to see things as they really are and, if I understand them today, it is because I have drawn nearer to the centre. If I stray away from the centre − if only for a couple of days − disorder begins to seem normal to me, too, and I begin to wonder what is so reprehensible about it. This is why I understand other people. The trouble is, though, that

they don't understand themselves; they don't know where they
stand or why. I know where they stand because everything in my
head is properly classified and filed where it belongs. I know
exactly where someone is standing and how near or how far he
is from the centre, from the divine world.

Ah, yes, this question of the centre and the periphery is so
important. I have often spoken to you about it and about the
symbol of the circle with the dot in the centre which we can see
in our eyes as well as in other parts of our body[2]. And yet, in
spite of the fact that human beings carry a symbolic form of this
'book of wisdom' permanently in their bodies, they have never
understood it. It has been a part of them for millions of years
but they have never learned to decipher it. The periphery and the
centre both exist and we must stay close, as close as possible, to
the centre, for only there shall we find peace. At the periphery
there is only confusion and disorder and the nearer you get to
it the more you are in danger of being flung even further from
the centre until you disintegrate in space. The centre represents
man's highest point, the apex of his being, his soul and spirit.
And the periphery represents the discord and difficulties that he
encounters when his consciousness strays off-centre and dwells
on all that is foreign and extraneous to his soul and spirit. Most
human beings spend their time swinging back and forth between
the centre and the periphery: a little peace and tranquillity followed by difficulties and disorder; again, a moment of peace,
and so on. Very few are capable of remaining immovably at the
centre, the peak of their being.

To illustrate this concept of the periphery and the centre, I
have often used the image of the 'Rotor', the spinning circular
platform that one sees in amusement parks. Of course, the Rotor
is just an amusement, but it is an excellent example of the effects
of the centrifugal and centripetal forces that exist not only on

2 See *Collection Izvor*, No 201, 'Towards a Solar Civilization'.

the physical plane but also in the spiritual life. If you don't want to be flung off-centre by centrifugal force you must constantly check your position and, if you find that you have drifted towards the periphery, remind yourself that you will suffer for it and then, without wasting time, get back to the centre.

When you see signs of chaos in your inner life, take it as a warning: sooner or later you are bound to be tripped up or ground to dust, to be knocked off balance and to hit or be hit by someone. This is how the law works. Of course, a doctor will explain your condition by saying that you are suffering from a lack or an excess of minerals or vitamins; a priest will say that it is because you don't go to church; your local politician will say that it is because you don't belong to his party, etc. They will all have their own theories about what ails you, but I can give you the real explanation — and it is very simple: it is because you have strayed from the centre. You may not understand what I am really saying, but this is the most accurate explanation; far more accurate than the explanations offered by doctors, priests or politicians because it sums up a whole philosophy.

The language I use comes from very far away and very high up. It is not the complicated language you use, with all those words and phrases I am obliged to adopt in order to make myself understood by you. I would far prefer to speak to you in my own language, the geometrical, cabbalistic, astrological language of symbols. But you don't know this language and none of you would understand me. I have to use your language and take examples from the things you see and experience in your everyday lives if I want you to understand me, but I still have my own special language. I know in advance that, if I tell someone, 'You're way off-centre, old man!' he will not understand, and yet it is the most accurate explanation for his difficulties. Try to understand, therefore, that we must constantly move closer to this centre within us. This is what we are doing here, every day, several times a day, through our meditations and spiritual exercises and, especially, every morning at sunrise[3].

As we come closer to the sun — symbolically speaking — we receive more light and greater warmth and life becomes more intense. Those who move away from the centre, from the spiritual sun, wonder why they are cold and in darkness, why life deserts them. I can tell them; it is very simple: 'You have strayed too far from the centre; you need to get back to it in order to find light, warmth and life.' 'But we *are* alive!' they protest. 'Oh no, you're not really alive; not yet! To be alive is to be luminous and warm and brimming over with blessings for all. Where are all those blessings?' No; human beings just don't know what life is. Everything is confused in their minds; the world is still a Tower of Babel and people don't understand each other.

Young people want to force their own language on me, but theirs is the language of anarchy and destruction whereas mine is the language of synarchy, order, happiness, joy and fulfilment. They ask me to adopt another language, the language of revolution, the language of Fidel Castro or Mao Tse-tung. But what sort of a language is that? I ask you! No, no! My language comes from another realm and I have my own yardstick by which to judge a person's behaviour. You see, I am showing you, little by little, where I find the measuring rods and scales, the slide-rules and calculators, the microscopes and telescopes I use and, before long, you will understand that you must adopt the same criteria. So come with me trustingly and without reserve, come with me quietly and I will take you to my laboratories where I weigh and measure everything, where I analyse everything in my test-tubes, just as a chemist analyses samples of blood or urine.

Yes, I have many instruments of this kind and I can see that human beings are drifting away from the centre. It is becoming

3 See *Complete Works*, vol. 10, 'The Splendour of Tiphareth', especially the first four chapters.

more and more rare to find people who manifest true greatness or nobility of character. More and more, the world is full of miserable creatures who spend their time chattering and running round in circles, creatures who have abandoned the light and replaced it with an indescribable clutter of aberrations and topsy-turvy ideologies. In a group of thirty people you will hear fifty different philosophies being expounded! The world is fast becoming one vast hospital: nobody sees eye to eye with his neighbour. Even in such basic things as air, light, warmth or food, what is good for some is bad for others and vice versa. Each member of a family is different, not in a good sense, but in having different weaknesses or illnesses. Let people be different, by all means, but on an ascending scale. Unfortunately, nowadays, people differ only in their type of malady: some have Spanish flu, others have typhoid or cholera — symbolically speaking — not to mention all the different kinds of fever! The whole family is feverish: father, mother and children, but each in a different way.

My dear brothers and sisters, I wonder if you are beginning to understand what I am saying. The young need to be up and doing; I have no quarrel with that, but what they do must be an improvement on what their elders have done and, at the moment that is not the case. At least adults go to work regularly. To be sure, they go on strike too, from time to time, but they do manage to keep the country going. Young people are delinquents by comparison. They want to control everything when they are not even capable of controlling themselves. Adults have a better attitude and the young should allow themselves to be guided by them. If, one day, young people are capable of doing better than their elders, then, by all means, let them start giving their advice, but not otherwise. It is not a question of age but of superiority. We must allow ourselves to be guided by someone who is truly superior to others even if he is very young. Old age does not give someone who is obtuse and narrow-minded the right to command others. Ability is the only thing that counts. How old was Jesus when the three Wise Men from the East knelt before

him with their gifts of gold, frankincense and myrrh? And how
old was he when he taught the doctors of the Law in the Temple?
For an Initiate, the only things that count are greatness of soul,
high-mindedness and purity.

As far as the students are concerned, by the very fact that
they have failed to manifest this greatness of soul, they have put
themselves in the wrong.

The Bonfin, July 15, 1968

V

If you tell me that young people have many good points, many qualities, I can only say that I am well aware of it — more so than you, no doubt. And if you say that they will change and that, in the future, they will produce something more worthwhile, that too, I know better than you. But I am speaking about today not about the future: my analysis concerns what is happening now. I could probably reveal many details about the future that would surprise you, but that is not the question. Before long, the student revolts will be forgotten and things will be back to normal. So, although I don't intend to dwell at length on the present situation — for it is no more than an episode and there will be others — I want to take the opportunity it gives me to explain certain laws to you for, if you don't start at once, in the future, when other, far more serious events occur, you will not know how to understand or react to them or which side you should be on. And this is extremely important for, when you choose a side, you are, as it were, casting your vote and your name goes down on record as a partisan of this or that movement. You have to know, therefore, what the different movements and currents are and what effects they will have.

One thing which is very important for human beings is to know exactly where they stand, who they are voting for and whose cause

they are serving. But the trouble is that they never take the trouble
to find out the correspondences and affinities between their decisions in this world and the realities of other spheres. And yet,
when you decide on a course of action, you are setting your train
on a particular track and, if you do so blindly, you may find that
your destination is not what you had bargained for. Yes, every
decision, on whatever subject, sets wheels in motion and, if you
don't know this, you will always be unhappy, always at the mercy
of other forces. You cannot be master of the situation if you are
blind. Knowing all this, I long to share my knowledge and experience with you so that you may benefit from them also. For life
is truly marvellous − but it would be even more marvellous if
you understood the underlying forces you set in motion and their
ramifications in other spheres.

Young people need a mentor who can reveal to them the meaning of life and how they can live it in such a way that all their
innate forces, qualities and talents may be made manifest in all
their fullness. If they learned this then, indeed, the young would
be a dazzling example to the world. But, as it is, they are on very
slippery ground. It is not enough to have read a few books and
earned a few diplomas in order to be more capable than others.
True capability in life is a question of character, not of school-
ing. Some people, who barely know how to read and write, possess extraordinary wisdom and understanding. People who have
a University degree are more and more inclined to think that others
should kowtow to them. But they are wrong: some things are
more important than book learning.

You will say, 'But it's not the fault of the poor students. It's
not they who decide the programme of studies or the degree re-
quirements'. That's true; I realize that, and I agree that all that
needs to be changed. The present system of education needs a thor-
ough spring-cleaning: the curriculum and exams need to be
changed; some disciplines should be dropped altogether; only the
essentials should remain, but, above all, the whole orientation
must be changed. I have always said that schools and universities

train the young to use their intellect in order to succeed at all costs in the world, to cheat and get the better of others but never to transform themselves. If they are ambitious, timid, proud, sensual or avaricious at the beginning of their studies, they will still be so at the end. But here we have a different kind of school to offer, a school in which, instead of learning to recite scientific formulae or lists of names and dates, the students study human nature and learn to change their character and transform themselves, to become better men and women. Unfortunately, there will never be very many candidates for our school because it is more difficult to work at one's own transformation than to learn the contents of a book by heart.

To be sure, instruction can win you prestige, money and a good job here on earth but it will not be much help to you in finding your way to other worlds. When you leave this world, the Heavenly beings who examine your credentials will not be impressed by your university degrees; they have other weights and measures by which to judge you. They will want to see how much love, kindness and light flows from you and, if they see that all your degrees and diplomas have only served to increase your pride and vanity — and this is so often the case — you will have to pay the penalty. One would have to be a second Dante to know which circle of Hell is destined to receive all the scholars and scientists who are so full of their own learning!

In the eyes of Cosmic Intelligence, human values are not the true values. Men weigh the pros and cons of a situation, make their decisions and command others on the strength of their own standards without ever wondering whether, in fact, they are not attaching too little or too much importance to certain values. The importance attributed to instruction is out of all proportion and yet, if you ask how long it takes to acquire a degree, you will find that it can be done in three or five years or, at the most, seven for a doctor. Does this seem long? Yes, perhaps; but how long does it take to acquire patience, kindness, generosity and wisdom? Not a few years but a few centuries! It is easy to earn a human degree but it takes hundreds of years to develop a few moral qualities. Isn't it illogical, therefore, to underestimate qualities that a man has worked so long to acquire?

Does learning make people better? Not at all; often, in fact, it does just the opposite. What is the point of a university education if it cannot make you a better person? Everybody wants to be rich; everybody wants success, glory and, above all, comfort and pleasure. But when the day comes for them to leave this earth, all their material and intellectual acquisitions will vanish without a trace. They will leave all that behind them and, when they come before the Heavenly beings awaiting them in the world above, they will be ashamed of the ugliness and obscurity they have amassed on earth. For my part, I have studied in a different school and it is in that school that I want to enrol you, too, so that you may work for something worthwhile, something that will last for all eternity. Then, when you come back to earth, instead of being destitute, you will bring many exceptional gifts with you.

If you want to make progress you must believe me. In any case, you will have to do so one day: when you get to the next world you will begin to believe what I am telling you today but, by then, it will be too late. You will only be able to regret your present attitude, thinking: 'How true it all was! Why didn't I believe him?' And then you will have to return to earth to repair all your mistakes. What a waste of time and effort! I am telling you the absolute truth and I am not alone in having experienced it; thousands of others have already done so. If there is one thing I am absolutely sure of, it is this. I have doubts about everything else, but this I know to be an absolute truth and it determines all my work and all my thoughts. Take away this truth and life has no meaning any more.

Well, one day you will believe me; of that I am sure. Wherever I go, people tell me that they feel that something is missing in their lives. Of course something is missing! The trouble is that they don't know what that something is and they always think that they'll find it in material possessions. No; the need they feel

comes from their soul and spirit but, as they refuse to acknowledge the existence of the soul and the spirit, they continue to
try to satisfy it by nourishing their physical body. But the nourishment of the physical body is not the nourishment craved by
the soul — nor by the heart or the intellect. I have already explained this in my lectures about the synoptic table[4].

As long as human beings refuse to open their minds and hearts
to infinity and eternity, to the realm of the soul and spirit, they
will always have this feeling of deep dissatisfaction. Of course,
it is obvious that they have never prepared themselves to find the
nourishment for which their soul and spirit crave; those who have
prepared themselves find what they need at once. You have all
seen how baby ducklings react: they are hardly out of the egg
before they tumble into the pond and begin to swim. Yes, because
they are equipped to do so! Animals that are not equipped in
the same way would simply drown. So, as human beings are not
equipped to find the nourishment they need for their soul and
spirit, they still have to learn, and that is what I am trying to do:
make them capable of recognizing and appreciating other values.
This is why you must help me to distribute the treasures of this
Teaching. It is such a shame that all this light should be useful
to only a handful of people. And even that handful is still too
busy with all kinds of work and activities that tie them down.
They have no time for the spiritual: they're too busy with other
things.

A great many people have said to me, 'All that you tell us
is so wonderful! Marvellous! I can feel that it is true, but I just
don't have the time — what with the family, my job, all our social
and business obligations, I have more than I can handle already!'
And they think that this is a valid excuse. But I have my own
methods for weighing and measuring things and I say that, if they
had a glimmering of intuition, if they had already been very advanced in the past, they would not have committed themselves to

4 See *Complete Works*, vol. 17, chap. 6.

so many obligations and activities and would not be in the plight
they are in today; they would have kept themselves free. The fact
that they are bound by so many obligations shows that they failed
to evolve sufficiently in previous incarnations to benefit, today,
from this marvellous science.

How is it that some people, even from a very early age, begin
to prepare themselves, feeling that they must keep themselves free
to serve the Lord, the Spirit, to serve mankind? It is because they
have a deep-seated memory of the past or because, before rein-
carnating, they promised their divine guides to be faithful to a
high ideal. I could tell you of many cases of this sort. Others
always think that they are justified in allowing themselves to be
caught in the grip of matter. They say, 'What can anyone do about
it, old man? That's life!' But, being a little more clear-sighted,
I say that they should not be so sure that their attitude is justified, for the fact that they are bogged down in material things
proves that they crave possessions and pleasure – and this shows
that they lack the light.

Forgive me for saying this, but truth is truth. The plight of
those who have allowed themselves to be bound hand and foot,
to be entangled and mired in matter bears witness against them.
They should have kept themselves free for a gigantic, solemn,
grand and glorious work. Why are they not there when they are
needed? It is the Gospel parable of the rich man's banquet all
over again: A rich man gave a great supper and invited many
guests. When the time came he sent his servant to summon those
who were invited but they all had an excuse. One had bought some
oxen and wanted to try them out; another had to go and see a
new plot of land; a third had just got married. Then the rich man
was very angry and sent his servants into the town to bring in
all the poor and the lame and the blind. And it was they who
ate and drank and enjoyed the banquet because the others, the
so-called 'elect' were not free. This is more or less what is happening today: very few people are free to devote themselves to the
divine work.

If people could only realize that happiness, fulfilment and liberation lie in the activities they are so afraid of, whereas the things
they have set their hearts on can bring them only disappointment
and bitterness! I have known many who were terrified of the Holy
Spirit but who would cheerfully drink with the Devil! They don't
know that they are being deceived by the Black Lodge which
sneaks into their unconscious mind and whispers, 'Watch out!
You never know what will happen if you get involved with the
light, with the Lord. Whereas with us you'll be alright; you'll
always have plenty to eat and drink.' And the poor creatures
believe them and end in great distress. It is time to put a stop
to this business. The Gospels tell us that the Kingdom of God
will not be won by the faint-hearted but by those who dare and,
in the Mysteries of ancient Egypt, adepts were told, 'Know, will,
dare and keep silent!' Of these four precepts, the most difficult
is 'dare'. A lot of people 'know'; a lot of people 'will', but not
many 'dare'. They are all too faint-hearted. When it comes to
some madcap adventure they are full of courage but, when it
comes to reaching out to and communicating with the Lord, they
are terrified.

The Bonfin, July 18, 1968

Chapter Four

Communism and Capitalism

I

No political system has ever proved to be wholly effective. Neither a monarchy nor an oligarchy, a democracy nor a republic has ever found the definitive solution. And this is simply because the system of government is not everything. If individuals are not conscious of their duty as citizens, if they don't understand that they must live in harmony with each other, a country will always be in chaos whatever the political regime. There will always be excesses, disorders and tribulations.

Symbolically, democracy represents government by the stomach. Can the desires, appetites and instincts of the masses be relied on to have an accurate appreciation of what is good and what is bad? No. They have been given the freedom to make known their demands but have they ever been known to use that freedom to demand the Kingdom of God and His Righteousness? No. Have they ever demanded light or love? No, again. The only thing the stomach and belly demand is more to eat and the freedom to vandalize everything and make everything dirty. The masses haven't got an exalted ideal because an exalted ideal requires a head and there is no head. Also, of course, the head must be enlightened, luminous and disinterested for, if the individual at the top has exactly the same instincts as the clamouring masses below, he will be worthless.

Initiates work for the Kingdom of God and His Righteousness
and the Kingdom of God is a monarchy. This means that all the
countries of the world should be organized on the pattern of the
universe whose king is God. Now, I am not saying that, in our
day, a monarchy would be preferable to a republic; no, I am
speaking on the level of principles. I have no objection to government by the populace as long as the populace is enlightened. If
it is not enlightened it should not govern. Similarly, if the head
is unenlightened, ignorant and cruel, it should not govern, either.
As a matter of fact, it is often the head, not the stomach, that
does the most damage. You must understand, therefore, that I
am speaking symbolically and that, in the realm of symbols,
everything is perfectly clear and mathematically exact. If you try
to understand the world of symbols – which is the world of principles – you will never go wrong. But human beings get everything
mixed up; this is why the world is still the Tower of Babel and
people cannot understand each other.

I want to talk to you, today, about the distribution of wealth
because a brother asked me about this yesterday, and I know that
it is a question that troubles most human beings.
    It should help you to understand the rightful order of things
if we look at the human body. Why the human body? Because
Cosmic Intelligence has conceived creation in such a way as to
leave clues and pointers throughout nature so that men might find
these clues and, by reflecting and meditating on them, be capable
of reconstructing all that this sublime Intelligence thought and
desired and planned. In this way, when we study plants, crystals,
the stars, rivers and mountains, the sun and the planets and, above
all, man and the pattern on which he is built, we can discover
the intentions of Cosmic Intelligence and the splendour and subtlety of Its designs.
    One of the things we see when we study a human being is that
every part of him demands something: the stomach demands
food; the ears demand sound; the eyes demand light, colours,

the sun; the mouth and nose, yes, and the sexual organs, too, they all clamour for something. Our whole body, therefore, is constantly asking for something and this is perfectly natural, marvellous. The only thing is that there has to be a head to guide, control and organize all this, otherwise the results would be catastrophic, for a man would eat and drink too much or too little, he would let himself get too hot or too cold, he would neither hear nor see the dangers that threaten him. It is right and normal for the body to make its demands, therefore, but the head must judge which demands must be satisfied and which should be denied and exactly when, where and how much to give. There is never any shortage of demands; they are always there, but what about the head? Where is the head that is supposed to distribute to each member what it needs in accordance with divine rules and in divine proportions?

I don't wish to criticize either monarchy or democracy; they both have their good and bad aspects. What interests me is the spiritual dimension of this question; this is why I say that for the members to clamour for what they want is normal and magnificent but that there must be a head capable of examining their demands and deciding whether they should be met or not. Whether it be inwardly, for an individual, or outwardly, for society as a whole, an enlightened head is needed to guide the members and correct any deviations. And the members must believe in that head and follow its lead.

The pattern on which the human organism was created by nature is our most reliable frame of reference. It reveals the roots of the distribution of wealth as we see it today and of all the contestations, jealousies and revolutions in the modern world. Actually, however far back you go in human history, you will find that this problem has always existed. Someone who was stronger or more skilful than his fellows would be a more successful hunter, for instance, and become richer by bringing back more game. The unequal distribution of wealth is considered unjust but, in fact, it is perfectly just. Nature abhors equality, uniformity, parity.

Since the Revolution of 1789, France's motto has been 'Liberty, Equality, Fraternity' but, in reality, equality doesn't exist in the universe. It is inequality that reigns. On no level of creation is there equality. You will protest, 'But we have made equality a law!' Yes, but a law is something theoretical and abstract; a text to hang on the wall. The fact is that equality exists nowhere; nature asks for diversity and diversity engenders inequality. Look at minerals, plants and animals: what variety! And human beings? Although you will occasionally find a person who looks exactly like someone else, there are always some differences, for instance, in the colour of the skin or hair and, in any case, in their hands, since they can always be distinguished by their finger prints.

The result of this diversity is that the faculties, tastes and aspirations of individuals are different and, consequently, that each one has different intellectual, emotional and physical capabilities. Some will accomplish noble deeds and win all the prizes in competitions or in the struggle for life, while others will always trail along behind because they haven't got the same capabilities. It is because of this difference in capabilities, therefore, that some human beings have more than others. Is this normal? Absolutely! Should we be indignant about it? Absolutely not! But people never think things through; they allow themselves to be led on by others and start shouting and protesting like everybody else. But the important thing for us, at the moment, is to study and understand the question and be very clear about it. If, on examination, we find that there is something to protest and fight about, very well; but first let's get it all quite clear.

However much people possess, it is normal and just. You will object, 'But they have got all that by exploiting and assassinating others'. Yes, that's true: man has a centuries-old tendency that drives him to gratify all his appetites. As time wore on, he saw that it was necessary to have a code of ethics – not that he had any real desire to be ethical, but it was to his advantage to have some rules for, if theft and murder were forbidden, he would be safer – but this moral code is still very far from perfect. Men still try to steal from others, to take what doesn't belong to them, if not on the physical plane (because on the physical plane one is always in danger of being found out and put in prison) on other, invisible, planes: people steal each other's thoughts and sentiments. The same old instincts are still manifesting themselves – more and more vigorously, in fact – but on other, subtler levels.

Everyone knows this today: you are all aware of the existence of industrial espionage, for example, by which companies try to obtain the secret plans or formulae of their business competitors. This is simply one manifestation of those age-old instincts of acquisitiveness and domination. It is impossible to get rid of these instincts and, if you do not know how to transform and sublimate them, you may prevent them from manifesting themselves on the physical plane, but they will only seek an outlet on the mental and astral planes. In this case, the crimes are the same but the form is different because it is invisible. As long as Initiation is not there to give a spiritual orientation to these forces, they will keep trying to manifest themselves. What can you expect? Ambition, sensuality and anger are formidable forces which must find an outlet.

The urge to compete and to possess more and more is absolutely normal. At what point does it become abnormal? Our own bodies tell us this so clearly that no philosopher could object. If I gave you only my own opinion, everyone else could say, 'No, no; that's not it at all! In my opinion it is thus and so...' and the argument would be endless. I'm not giving you a personal opinion, therefore; I'm giving you the opinion of Nature herself – and this is something that you are obliged to accept – and you will see how she has solved the problem through us.

The question is this: 'Is it legitimate to amass wealth?' And the answer is: 'Of course it is!' What does the stomach do when you give it some food? It immediately takes possession of all that it needs and sends the rest on elsewhere; it doesn't keep what it doesn't need. In fact, even what it does take is not used only for itself; it processes it and distributes it to the rest of the body. The stomach only keeps what it needs for a few hours; after a few hours it feels the need for more food so it eats again. And this is what keeps a man healthy and enables him to talk and move about and work and sing, etc. But suppose that the stomach were to say, 'From now on I'm going to keep everything I can get for myself. Why should I keep giving what I have to those idiots? What do they matter? There could be a famine any day now; you never know what the future holds, and I have a big family to look after.' So it starts keeping everything for itself and, in no time at all, it is very ill, simply because it has broken the law of impersonal[1] unselfishness and brotherhood. And then you have a tumour or a cancer or whatever else you like to call it. And the same thing applies to the lungs, the head and any other organ.

Human beings are all cells of a single body. In fact, the number of cells in our own bodies is far greater than the number of human beings on earth; the brain alone contains billions of cells. And if all these billions of cells in our bodies manage to live happily together as a family, how is it that human beings are too stupid to achieve the same harmony and unity and have never managed to do away with the barriers that separate them? If only they could achieve this universal brotherhood, there would be such prosperity that neither countries nor individuals would ever feel the need to hoard their wealth and defend it against others; there would always be enough of everything for everyone.

If human beings are now so eager to accumulate as much as possible, it is because they have got themselves into an inextricable situation which obliges them to foresee and insure themselves

---

1 This use of the word 'impersonal' may be misunderstood if it is not placed in the context of Omraam Mikhaël Aïvanhov's teaching concerning the two natures in man, the human and divine, the lower self and the higher Self or, as he calls them, the personality and the individuality. For a fuller treatment of the subject, See *Complete Works*, vol. 11, 'The Key to the Problems of Existence' and *Collection Izvor*, No. 213, 'Man's Two Natures, Human and Divine'.

against the threat of disaster. In other conditions no one would feel the need to hoard because everyone would have all they need; even public transport would be free. People would continue to work so as not to get rusty, but they would work without being paid. Yes, they wouldn't ask to be paid because it would be so pleasant to be surrounded by people who reward you for your work by their gratitude and smiles, by their love. Money becomes insignificant in comparison. With the philosophical system in which human beings live, today, there can never be any real improvement: even if political regimes change, the same madmen and the same assassins will still be there; human tragedies will be the same, and human blood will continue to be spilled.

So, as you can see, I am in favour of wealth; it is necessary. The only thing is that I have never looked for wealth on the physical plane because, on this plane, it is a burden. You always have to think about it in order to keep it, and that means a life of suspicion and anxiety. Wealth is fine, but it never leaves you in peace for one minute. And not only that: if you are weak, sensual or vindictive, it can very quickly make a wreck of you, morally and even physically, because it makes it possible for you to indulge yourself to excess. Yes, wealth is good, but you have to be very strong if you are to put it to good use.

And what about poverty? Well, poverty is not so marvellous either, for the poor are always humiliated and obliged to submit to others; they can never fulfil their noblest aspirations. Poverty is not really very wonderful. In fact, if St Francis of Assisi came back today, he would get hardly anyone to follow him. Everything is very different now; times have changed. In St Francis' day, men were capable of living in constant awareness of the divine world and of eternal life; today, they are so deeply plunged into the world of matter and so avid for comfort and ease that, no matter how much you talk to them about Heaven, no one is interested.

In the past, the poor were quite ready to accept that others were rich. In fact, the belief was deeply rooted in the soul of the people that, if God gave a man wealth, it was because he deserved it; no one found anything to quarrel with in that. Wealth, like intelligence and beauty, was considered a gift and no one questioned a person's right to it. But nowadays, as soon as someone has a little more than his neighbours, they are all there, saying, 'Why? Why him? Why not me?' Even if someone is a nonentity, a complete bungler, he still thinks he has every right. Yes, this is how it is today, and this is why we see wise men living in poverty while fools strut about in luxury.

And yet poverty is a blessing for those who are wise enough to understand it for it allows them to evolve, to advance on the path that leads to God. Those who are uninterested in approaching the Deity want everything they can get here and, because their ambition is for the things of the earth, for material possessions, their life is a constant series of quarrels, turbulence and crime. A wise man will never start a revolution in order to become rich. On the contrary, he will say, 'If people only knew how rich I am! I'm as rich as Croesus. Richer than Midas! Everything I touch turns to gold.' And all the other poor wretches, who have no idea how to become spiritually rich, spend their time fighting each other for material possessions.

Now, none of this means that I think employers have the right to exploit workers. No, those who exploit others are not intelligent either. Look at the way the cells of our bodies behave: they don't try to exploit each other; on the contrary, they all try to help each other. When one organ is deficient, another one compensates in order to restore the balance. Some really extraordinary examples of this have been seen.

I realize, of course, that what I am saying may not be understood; it is not possible, in the space of an hour and a half, to say everything that needs to be said about problems that have never ceased to torment mankind. But I can try, at least, to get you to reflect on them.

From my point of view, true wealth is in the realm of the soul and the spirit; this is where I look for it. And I know that, if

I have that wealth, I shall also have material wealth: it will come
to me of its own accord. Of course, for the time being, this cor-
respondence between inner and outer wealth cannot be seen here,
on earth. And yet it is a cosmic law: external wealth must correspond to inner wealth and external poverty must correspond
to inner poverty. In nature, this is so: the animals, plants and
minerals that contain a wealth of chemical, nutritional and medical
properties are also outwardly rich in matter, form and colour.
But, because they have free will, human beings have diverted and
distorted things and those who are inwardly richer than others
in patience, love, intelligence, generosity and purity are often outwardly poorer. And those who are poorest in qualities and virtues are the richest in outward things.

Actually, as this law cannot lie, we can sometimes see its
manifestation in people's faces or bodies. Every lofty, luminous
thought and every harmonious sentiment creates corresponding
geometrical forms. And every dark thought and unbridled pas-
sion creates chaotic forms. This is why those who possess intelligence, love and purity will always attract to themselves gold and
precious stones and all that is best in creation. Believe me: this
is a universal law. And the others, those who are inwardly poor,
dirty and decrepit will always attract conditions that correspond
to their inner state. This, too, is the law. You may say, 'Oh, that's
a great consolation!' but, in point of fact, you shouldn't even
think about that; you should only think about working to acquire
spiritual wealth so as to be in a position to help others and to
heal, console and guide them. Every other kind of wealth is a
burden.

Remember the lecture in which I told you that, even in the
midst of his quest for pleasure, what man is really looking for
is God. The trouble is that he looks for him in the cesspools of
life instead of at the Source. Those who are fond of women or
drink are looking for God; those who are fond of gold are also
looking for God, but they are looking on too low a level, in the
metal. The mistake human beings always make is to look for God

in such remote and bizarre forms that they hinder their evolution. They hanker for gold because they know that gold can give them everything else. To be sure, they also know — or, at least, they have been told — that God is the fulfilment of all their needs and desires, but He is a bit too abstract; they can't see Him. There is nothing very tangible to hang on to when you possess God whereas, when you possess gold, you only have to say, 'I want this or that', and it's yours. Thanks to your gold, you can order other people about and have whatever you want; you can be happy and contented — or discontented, but that's another story!

And now, what does Initiatic Science tell us? That gold is nothing more than the light of the sun that has been condensed in the bowels of the earth for millions of years. Those who hanker for gold do so because they have a faint, inner intuition that what they are looking for is the light of the sun, which contains both life and love. They are perfectly right to seek wealth, therefore, and all the more so if they seek the wealth of light because, in doing so, they are going straight to what they want, whereas others take a roundabout way to reach it.

Man has an instinctive hunger for gold because he senses that there is something divine, a hidden essence, in it. But an Initiate doesn't look for gold, he looks for light. He says, 'Instead of hunting for gold in the depths of the earth, I go directly to light, knowing that that light will condense into gold within me and I shall become pure gold'. Isn't that much better than having piles of gold in your pockets or your cupboards? You will say that you have never seen a golden Initiate. Of course not; his gold is all inside him. It is his light and it is there even if you can't see it. 'And what can he do with that gold?' you ask. My goodness, how ignorant you are! Don't you know that in the world above there are 'shops' in which his gold buys wisdom, peace and joy? Whereas those who are materially wealthy, in spite of all their precious metal, are harassed and unhappy, eaten away by rot and mould. All their gold is not sufficient to make them happy. Do you understand what I am saying or not? There are things that you don't know and that you must know; and not only must you know them but you must live in such a way as to obtain them. There is a whole science here. Perhaps you will say that that is all a lot of nonsense. Well, nonsense or not, it works!

Do you want to know how an Initiate spends his gold? Well, when someone is ill, for instance, it means that he has done wrong and is paying for his faults, so I tell the Heavenly entities, 'I love this person because he has been generous to the Brotherhood. How much does he owe?' Then I pay his debt and he immediately gets better. Believe me, these things are real; this gold can be used to pay for someone else and obtain a cure. So, as you see, it is good to look for wealth, but you must look for it where it truly exists in its quintessence and not only in the dense, crystallized form in which it is virtually useless. It is not in that form that it can give you what is essential. If you had to pick up your strong-boxes and carry them across a desert, you would soon be calling on the Lord to send someone to rescue you. You would willingly exchange the money in your coffers for a glass of water. But, if no help came, you would die of thirst, still in possession of all your gold. Whereas, if you have the other kind of gold, you wouldn't have to die because you could drink and quench your thirst.

There is no other way: light is the only solution. This is why human beings must be taught this truth so that, one day, they lose the urge to hoard. When mankind becomes one family and national barriers disappear, this need will also disappear and there will be no more injustice. Universal brotherhood is the only solution: universal brotherhood as we see it in our own bodies. Today, with all the wars that are going on, the body of the world is ill; it needs to be purified for it is suffering from constipation, diarrhoea and anything else you like to mention. Above all, it is suffering from cancer, for cancer is simply the consequence of the philosophy of violence and anarchy that is so prevalent today.

No matter what they attempt, there will be no solution to the problem of wealth as long as human beings have needs that they are unable to control. Even Communism cannot provide the solution. Ideas are all very well, but until human beings are sufficiently selfless to live a divine life, even the best ideas are bound to degenerate. Look at how Christianity has degenerated and become materialized. Although human beings must be led forward to new horizons, as long as they are too deeply immersed in matter there is nothing one can do about it; they refuse to budge.

The Bonfin, July 11, 1968

II

This question of the distribution of wealth torments many
people. They cannot accept that some should be rich and others
poor. But that is reality. In nature, inequality is the rule: some
are poor and others are rich. Why do people imagine that they
should all be equal? Equality would only mean stagnation; there
would be no movement, no evolution, because there would be
no incentive to compete. Besides, isn't God rich? Of course He
is; He is the richest Being in all the universe, and Communists
must be very disgruntled at not being able to rob Him of His
wealth. It's probably because they consider Him a Capitalist that
they have done away with Him!

This whole question of wealth really needs to be straightened
out. People are deeply troubled and unhappy about it and kill
themselves trying to change the situation, but they will never succeed, never; for nature endorses inequality. Why should we take
pity on those who are lazy, incompetent and ignorant? To show
them a little generosity is one thing, but to give exactly the same
to people who are stupid and ignorant as to those who have great
talent and learning is quite simply unjust. Capitalists may be
dishonest but Communists are unjust. So, dishonesty or injustice
– there is really not much to choose between them. They are
all tarred with the same brush!

Much more light is needed, that's all; if there were much more light and love everything would sort itself out. But you must never count on force or violence. The only way to make people better is to get them to understand how many unhappy consequences a dishonest or unjust act can have and to learn to put themselves out for others and take pleasure in doing so. Without this, whatever political regime is in power, you will never make society any better.

Whether it be in the area of wealth, power or knowledge, you will never do away with competition. Why prevent people from becoming rich? If not materially, at least spiritually rich in qualities and virtues. Personally, I consider myself rich. Does that mean that you have to set up a howl and come and massacre me, because I'm rich? Of course, my wealth is not financial, but that doesn't prevent me from feeling rich and, above all, rich in understanding. I understand other people's situation and all their difficulties and failings and I'm ready to excuse them all – even readier than they are. 'If that is so', you will say, 'Why are you always berating them and demanding a greater effort?' Ah, that is simply my educational method; I am trying to get them to improve. But, in reality, I understand their difficulties and distress perfectly, because I have known all that they are going through; the Invisible World wanted me to experience the same problems so that I could understand others. If someone tells me, 'Sir, I haven't eaten for three days', I'm not one to reply, 'Make an effort, my good man; make an effort!' and go on my way without giving him something. No, I know what it is; I have known every sort of privation, illness, insult and humiliation. The Invisible World has prepared me very thoroughly to understand anything and everything. But, because my role is to educate human beings, I don't show it. I show them that I expect a great deal of them.

I shall never prevent anyone from seeking wealth. I simply tell those who do so what they must do to avoid being crushed under an unbearable burden of worry, fear, anxiety and suspicion. For this is inevitable when one does not possess the light. So, you must be rich, but without falling a prey to all the negative states of mind that dog those who follow this path; you must be rich, but not at the expense of your neighbour and, above all, you must see that your wealth circulates and take pleasure in letting others share in it. Why don't I keep all that I have learned for myself? I share it with others because it makes me happy to do so. If I hoarded my harvest of knowledge and experience, mice and mildew would attack it and not a grain would be left. That is why I hasten to plant all my seeds. If the rich could only do the same, if only they could find it in them to say, 'I have all this and I'm going to share it with others', they would become so exalted and noble and so happy. Yes, to give is a way of making progress. But people are not in the habit of giving. Many people possess billions and keep it all for themselves and, in addition, they are utterly miserable. People need to learn to share their wealth, but they must never be prevented from becoming rich.

In any case, remember that I have foretold what will happen: given the Law of Correspondences which decrees that inner wealth ultimately leads to outer wealth, he who has an inner store of precious stones — a treasury of virtues — will one day have the same precious stones outwardly: rubies, turquoises, topazes, jaspers, diamonds and sapphires, etc. If this is not yet the case, it is because those who are inwardly rich are not greedy for possessions and those who are take everything for themselves. There is nothing left for one whose only thought is for Heaven, for perfection. When I was very young I read a poem by Schiller that filled me with delight. It spoke of the beginning of the world: the Lord had just finished sharing out His creation. The forests and lakes, fields, rivers and mountains had all been distributed when along comes the poet with his lyre. 'Lord', he asks, 'Is there anything left for me?' 'My poor fellow', exclaims the Lord, 'I have given everything away. There's nothing left. Where were you?' 'Oh, I was under that tree, over there; I was contemplating the heavens and singing Your praises.' 'In that case' said the Lord,

'The heavens are yours!' And this is always true: the heavens are always open to a real poet. Others have all the rest, but he is richer than any of them, for the heavens belong to him.

Yes, wealth is a problem: it has always been a cause of division and strife between human beings. Countless family tragedies have been caused by an inheritance, for instance. Rapacity is always the rule... no wonder the world never manages to shake off its miseries! All wars stem from the ambition to own more, to possess something — money or land — that belongs to one's neighbour. If people knew how to be generous, all these problems would be solved. We must be rich and we must distribute our wealth. No one is richer than the Lord, and His representative the sun is so rich that his wealth overflows and pours from him; if he didn't distribute his wealth he would burst. Why not imitate the sun? In doing so you would solve every problem: there would be no more Capitalists and no more Communists, only children of God, admiring and delighting in each other.

The Bonfin, July 19, 1968

III

Some so-called philosophers would like to abolish man's desire for wealth. But this is not possible: they will never succeed, for it is Nature herself who has given man the desire to be rich, if not on the physical plane, then on the emotional or intellectual plane. Man has the innate urge to enrich himself in one way or another on every plane of being. It is exactly the same with his tendency to make war: that, too, will never be abolished for that, too, is an instinct fostered and nourished by Nature. If Nature has given man a head, it was so that he would use it not to wipe out his instincts but to give them direction and put them to good use.

Almost all the rewards of society — prestige, social prominence, influence and authority — are based on wealth. A warmer welcome and greater deference is always shown to the rich, even if they are dishonest. Even the chief of a tribe of savages has something more or better than the others: a few more feathers or more statues, a few more little pots. It is Nature herself that gives human beings the instinct to do better than others. The only trouble is that, if the head is not in charge, they are inclined to exaggerate and be unjust and to break the law. But when the head is in control, that is to say, when they are lucid and use their reason, all their instincts — their acquisitive instinct, the instinct to compete and do better than others, the instinct of aggression, even the sexual instinct — all these instincts can develop normally. For they are forces, useful impulses that urge men to advance.

Of course, when human beings are too primitive they are not capable of intervening in their own inner life or of harmonizing, controlling and guiding their instincts. History gives us many examples of this. Personally, I am not in favour of abolishing men's instincts because, when you do that, you abolish all that stimulates them, life comes to a standstill and all progress ceases. A lot of people say that we should destroy such and such a vice or uproot such and such a tendency. But that is no solution, for Nature will continue to produce other individuals with the same tendencies. A programme of destruction is doomed from the start. We destroy snakes and mosquitoes but Nature simply produces more the following year. This is why the old methods have never produced good results: they were applied without wisdom. Wisdom lies in acknowledging the intelligence of Nature, in deferring to her and, in this way, becoming capable of understanding her designs and the reasons for them.

If we ask Nature how she envisages things, she will say, 'What about you? How do you build a ship? You put engines into it, but are the engines intelligent? No, they drive the ship forward but they are perfectly capable of driving it onto the rocks or into an iceberg or bringing it into collision with another ship and wrecking the whole thing.' 'Yes, but there is always a captain on board. He is intelligent and he keeps his eyes open and steers the ship.' 'Exactly! When I created man, I gave him engines to drive him forward, and those engines often spit fire, but I also gave him a captain. The only trouble is that the captain has gone to sleep, or perhaps he is drunk and has abandoned his post and the whole ship is drifting out of control.' 'Oh, how simple the whole thing is! And to think that I wanted to stop the engines!' 'No, keep the engines running, but wake up the captain because the poor fellow has lost his grip.' The engines are below decks, in the bowels of the ship and above, in the head, is the captain who uses your eyes, ears and mouth to look and listen and give his orders. Why is your head not between your legs, for instance, or on the soles of your feet? Actually, that is where a lot of people keep it — symbolically speaking. Anarchists, who refuse to reason, sacrifice everything to the engines and disdain the head. Try talking to them about wisdom, order or intelligence and you will see their reaction. What they advocate is blind brute force.

Of course, Mars will always exist and human beings will always feel the need to fight and conquer. The goal and the means will change but the need, the tendency, will never disappear. You have the right to declare war on the whole of humanity, but only with the weapons of love and light. The day will come when human beings will no longer wage war. You will say, 'But you are contradicting yourself!' No; I am saying that war as we know it today, with all the destruction that this implies, will not exist in the future. Human beings will eventually understand how costly it is and stop slaughtering each other. But, as the instinct for war will always be alive — Cosmic Intelligence Itself does not wish it to be destroyed — human beings will continue to fight each other in different ways and the conqueror, instead of bringing death and destruction to his adversaries, will give them life, wealth, light and love. How marvellous it will be! So, there will always be battles, but of a better kind... like the battles between the stars and the suns in which the weapons are arrows of light.

I have searched the Sacred Scriptures of all religions and found many noble, pure and luminous figures in them, but I have never found one to compare with the sun for light, love, generosity and perfection. The sun is the only being that expresses on earth the greatness of God, and it is the sun that I have chosen as my model. I love and respect all the others but I find that they all have their limits. If human beings are always so weak, lack-lustre, vindictive and forlorn, it is because their ideal is not something infinite. Their ambition is to be like their uncle or their neighbour or a noted politician or billionaire. What sorry models! Look at the disease and disorder of their lives! Whereas the sun... nothing can be compared to the sun and, however strange you find it, I have adopted it as my model. You will say, 'But no one can ever resemble the sun.' You're absolutely right; I know that better than you, but that doesn't matter.

If you take the sun as your model, little by little, your intellect will receive its light, your heart its warmth and your spirit its power. And, above all, you will give and give, as the sun gives. The guiding rule with human beings is to take; this is how they are brought up and the whole of contemporary civilization is marked by this need to take. It is the only word people understand.

One day a peasant fell into a well. A man, who happened to be passing by, heard him calling for help and, leaning over the edge of the well, he said, 'Give me your hand'. As soon as the peasant heard the word 'give' he withdrew the hand he had stretched out; he preferred to stay in the well rather than give something. When his rescuer realized that he was dealing with an inveterate miser to whom the word 'give' was anathema, he said, 'Here, take my hand'. Ah, the effect of the word 'take' was magical! The man immediately grasped his rescuers hand and was saved. He liked the sound of the word 'take' but not the word 'give'. And he is not the only one of his kind. Wherever you go, human beings are interested only in what they can take. They study, they work, they get married and go to parties or meetings always with one aim, that of taking, acquiring something. Their minds are always turned towards this. And this is why man no longer emanates light and warmth wherever he goes: because his only preoccupation is to see what he can take.

Even in love, when a man and woman come together, they are only interested in what they can get from each other: the man is bent on sucking life from the woman and vice versa. This is why it is better that they should separate, for they are transgressing the law of love. You will say, 'But they were truly together; they were really united'. Yes, but only with a view to what they could get out of it: each thought only of taking something from their partner, of feeding on him unscrupulously and without mercy. Instead of trying to sow something good — an impulse, some life, some inspiration — in his heart and soul so that he might awaken and advance... Oh, no; their only aim is to take, to eat and drink all they can and drain their partner dry. It is because of this mentality that the whole world is rushing towards destruction.

The only school that teaches people to give is the school of the sun. All the planets take. Only the sun gives and this is why we have to enrol in his school. He is the only one who really knows how to give; when we see this, how is it possible not to love him? We always love and are drawn to those who are capable of giving something good. Whereas, with those who are only capable of taking... Well, we soon learn to avoid them. Why do some people imagine that they will always be allowed to plunder others? The others soon see what they are like and leave them strictly alone. You must cultivate in yourselves a tendency to give.

The Bonfin, July 12, 1968

IV

The whole of the modern world is divided into two camps with Capitalists on one side and Communists on the other. Actually, Capitalism and Communism are not simply two different attitudes concerning the ownership of the means of production and the distribution of material wealth; they are much more than that.

Take the example of a young girl: in the past — and even, to a certain extent, today — a young girl starts out as a capitalist. She gives no one the right to kiss or fondle her: her charms are her own private property. Her parents have always told her she should be a capitalist and, for a time at any rate, she follows their advice. But, as the notion of communism spreads, it infiltrates every domain and, eventually, works its way into the mind of this young girl who begins to want to share her beauty and all the charms of her body with others. She has become a communist. It is no different for a boy who wants to make love to every girl: he, too, is a communist and distributes his quintessence to others. Yes, indeed; all that is a form of communism. Of course, I know that no one else understands it like this; I'm the only one who is sufficiently 'deformed' to see these things. This is why I say that Eskimos are more communistic than anyone, because, when a stranger visits them they lend him their wives.

Let's say, then, that a girl who gives away her capital to the first comer is a communist. Yes, but why does she give away her capital? So as to rob the boy of his. That kind of communism is not very honest. The girl becomes very sweet and generous, true, but only in order to get her hands on the boy's capital, because no one can survive without capital.

A young girl possesses considerable capital, therefore, and with it she can buy all kinds of things or, at the very least, get an invitation to a restaurant for a good meal — after which it is she who will be 'eaten'. But, let's say no more about that! As you can see, it is all quite complicated.

The truth is that Nature shows us that capitalism and communism are both necessary. What is a child? A capitalist. He screams to be given whatever takes his fancy and wants to keep it all for himself. But one day, when he marries and has children of his own, he will be obliged to become a communist; it will be his turn to start sharing out his wealth. It is Nature herself who obliges us to be both capitalists and communists at different periods of our lives. We begin by being capitalists, for we have to become rich. If you want to help others, you must be rich; how can you help anyone if you possess nothing? You can't: if you are too poor, you can't even help your own wife and children. You have to be rich in order to help others. Nature has given men all kinds of capital: their arms and legs, their eyes and ears, their genitals and their brains are all capital assets which they must put to work to earn riches which they can then share with others. Capitalism must be no more than a means, and the great mistake of Capitalists is to have made it an end in itself. In other words, Capitalists understand nothing about Capitalism — nor Communists about Communism, for that matter. You will soon see why.

Do Communists really and truly practise communism? The Lord alone knows! If they are so eloquent in their condemnation of Capitalists and so ready to combat them, it is often because they would like to be as rich and powerful as them. Personally, I believe in communism. Why? Because Jesus was a communist, but a white communist, not a red communist. Communists and

Capitalists alike should be instructed in an Initiatic school, for neither group thinks nor acts correctly. When you make wealth your goal, your ideal, all kinds of unforeseen problems result. On the other hand, if you practise communism without discernment, it will lead to other, equally dire results. If Communists and Capitalists refuse to be instructed in the light of the Teaching of the Universal White Brotherhood, they will massacre each other and civil war will pave the way for other wars. Neither group possesses the light that we can give them and that would enable them to work for a high ideal. They are working only for themselves; even when they seem to be working for others, in reality it is only for themselves.

Communists and Capitalists must understand each other in order to help mankind. Both are necessary, for the two currents of capitalism and communism are at work simultaneously in the universe. Why do human beings make these two currents a cause for division as though the balance of the whole universe did not rest on them? Each side does its best to eliminate the other. They talk and talk, and the poor ignorant fools who know no better swallow all their stupid theories.

To keep everything for oneself is one philosophy; to give everything to others is another philosophy. But neither philosophy is the right one: there is a third solution. Both capitalists and communists must give all that they possess, that is to say, their ideas and thoughts and all their work, to a third principle, a principle that is divine. Communists are ready to give, to be sure, but they give to human beings, and that doesn't really settle anything, for human beings are weak, fickle and ungrateful. And now, if we come back to the example of the young girl that I mentioned earlier, what conclusion can we draw? The conclusion that, instead of keeping everything for herself and being a capitalist or of distributing everything and being a communist, she should begin by becoming rich and giving everything to the Lord. Because the Lord is the only one who can advise her and tell her how much capital to distribute and how, when and whom to give it to.

Nowadays, everybody is eager for instruction and education so as to earn money and be respected and admired, for all doors are open to the rich and educated, and this is just one more manifestation of man's everlasting partiality for capitalism; that is to say, for possessions, property and positions of authority. To be sure, this urge takes different forms: some want wealth, others want knowledge. Knowledge belongs to a higher order, perhaps, but the tendency is always the same: to be rich so as to have a monopoly and dominate others. Yes, those who are very knowledgeable behave exactly like the rich, like capitalists: they are aloof and hostile. As for communists, they are the ignorant, disinherited paupers of the world. They huddle together to share their miserable lot, their crusts of bread, their bottles of cheap wine, their cigarette butts. Yes, it is an advantage for the poor to share with others but, if ever they become rich, look out! There will be no more sharing, no more communism; they will instantly cut themselves off from everyone else. When people are poor they are communists and when they are rich they are capitalists because, if they continued to be communists, they would have to share their wealth and they have not the least desire to share any of it. If you want millions of people to flock round you, there is nothing easier: all you have to do is invite all the beggars and vagrants to eat and drink, and they will come. The rich will never come.

All those who are ignorant, weak and poor have communistic tendencies; they like to invite each other, to be together, to hug and kiss. They are very accessible, very warm and friendly, because they have nothing. Whereas it's impossible to get near the pundits of the intellectual world. If you want to see them you have to ask for an appointment months in advance and, even then, they won't always give you one: they are unapproachable. They behave exactly like the rich. But this is all wrong: those who are rich in capacities and knowledge must not hold themselves aloof like haughty potentates, they must be friendly and brotherly and share their wealth. In this way they will be genuine communists.

If they seek knowledge, they should do so as a means to help their fellow men and not simply for their own benefit.

When I listen to all the political orators who make speeches on television, I can see that, whether they are Communists or Capitalists, they all have a capitalistic attitude: they all feel secure in their knowledge and confident of the force of their arguments; they are all despots; they have no love, no humility, no gentleness. Believe me, it's impossible to pull the wool over my eyes. I know exactly what category each attitude belongs to. You will say, 'But how can you class all these attitudes as communistic or capitalistic?' Ah, that is simply because everyone uses these wretched words so often. I could find others but, in the meantime, I find it very convenient to use these.

You must have knowledge, degrees and diplomas, but not for you, not solely for your own advantage. Knowledge must not be simply a gratification of your lower self. The wealth of talents you cultivate in order to become a scientist, an artist, a politician, etc., must be seen as a means by which to do good. In this way it becomes divine, because the two currents combine: you are both communist and capitalist. I have given a great deal of thought to this question over the years and, believe me, I have solved the problem: I have become the greatest communist alive and, at the same time, the greatest capitalist.

Capitalism and communism are both necessary and indispensable; Nature herself endorses both tendencies. A child who grabs everything for himself is a capitalist and an old man who distributes his possessions before leaving for the next world is a true communist: he keeps nothing for himself. Between these two extremes are all kinds of people who truly belong to neither category: capitalists who are not real capitalists and communists who are not true communists. The ideal situation is to be both at once, that is to say, to receive, earn and be enriched by all the splendours of Heaven and, then, to distribute them to one's fellow human beings. You must be a capitalist by amassing the things of Heaven, therefore, and a communist by distributing them on earth. This is perfection! But if you are only a communist or only a capitalist, you are lost, for that is too narrow, too restricted.

Communists and Capitalists are both right. People have a right to want private property; Nature has given them this right. A person's physical body, for instance, is his own property and it is dangerous to distribute it. There are certain things he can distribute, of course, but he must keep his body for himself. Look at a tree: a tree is both capitalist and communist because it keeps its roots, trunk and branches, but it distributes its fruit. This is the way Nature conceives things. An Initiate, who understands Nature's lesson, does exactly what a tree does: he retains possession of his roots, trunk and branches and distributes his fruits, that is to say, his thoughts and sentiments, his words and his light, his strength and his money. Only an Initiate is both a true communist and a true capitalist. Other men are quarrelsome children who have no understanding of the true life and this is why they will never find the solution to all their problems: because they do not possess the true light of Initiatic Science.

So, as you see, the true capitalist is an Initiate; he gets richer and richer every day. And he is also a true communist, for he spends his days and nights distributing his fruits. But he keeps his capital, for he could do nothing without it. Suppose someone comes to me and says, 'What a magnificent violin you have; do give it to me!' If I'm a true capitalist, I will say, 'No, I won't give you my violin; it's my private property. But you can come here every day and I'll play it for you.' But young people, girls and boys, give away their violin — their heart — and then, when they have lost it, they weep and wail, 'What have you done with my heart?' But they should never have given it away! A poor girl gives her heart to a boy who is so clumsy that the first thing he does is drop it. And then she cries because her heart is broken. If she had had any sense she would have known that the boy didn't need two hearts. In Bulgaria we say that you cannot carry two water melons under one arm. Keep your hearts, therefore – don't give them to anyone but the Lord – but distribute your sentiments to others. This is the best way to understand things.

As I was saying, the whole world is caught up in this division between Communists and Capitalists. People are always arguing and abusing each other; worse: countless crimes of theft and arson, bombings, kidnapping and assassinations are carried out because of these two words.

Communists are proud of their philosophy; they feel generous and altruistic. But, as they know nothing about the structure of human beings, they don't know that to improve their material conditions while rejecting all their spiritual aspirations can only result in disaster. In the long run, they become dishonest, deceitful and cruel – animals. A Communist who fails to cultivate his spiritual, mystical dimension, ends by becoming as bad as the worst Capitalist: unjust, violent, authoritarian and always ready to misuse his strength and power. So many examples are there to show that, in spite of their magnificent philosophy, a great many Communists end by betraying their principles. Yes, because it is easy to adopt an ideal philosophy, but it is much more difficult to put it into practice in one's everyday life; and yet that is the one thing that is essential. Cosmic Intelligence has designed human beings in such a way that they cannot reach perfection unless they maintain ties with a higher world which alerts them to possible dangers and gives them light and strength. A man who relies exclusively on his own limited intellect can neither foresee nor fully understand events, with the result that he makes catastrophic mistakes in every area. All those for whom power lies in technology, industry and material progress and who imagine that, because they have all these things at their command, even God is going to obey them, are bound, sooner or later, to bite the dust. When their conduct is inspired exclusively by their desire to lord it over everyone else and ignores the intentions of Cosmic Intelligence, they stir up certain layers of the physical and psychic atmosphere and provoke the hostility of fearful powers and forces which unleash a terrible reaction.

There are some tremendous surprises in store for political thinkers and heads of State who decide to solve problems without studying the underlying nature of man. For the need for spiritual nourishment will awaken in the breasts of the oppressed with such force that nothing, neither threats nor prisons nor death, will persuade them to give it up. And this will come about in the near future. This is why Russia faces the choice between being attacked by other powerful and well-armed powers or changing its attitude and replacing its form of communism by the true communism of Christ, the communism of the Universal White Brotherhood. When Russia does this it will be playing a truly glorious role because it will bring a new culture and a new spiritual civilization to the whole world.

I know, of course, that, for several years, Russia has been conducting research into parapsychological phenomena. But what is the purpose of this research? They are trying to find out if these means can be used to detect the thoughts and plans of others and emit waves to influence them and act on their minds. In this way, they hope to be able to subject others to their own will and get them to serve their interests. Obviously, the people who do this have no knowledge of Initiatic Science. As long as their only aim is to dominate other countries – even to the point of trying to kill people by sending them objects impregnated with noxious emanations – it proves that they are only interested in gratifying their lower, destructive, demonic nature. And this is black magic. I have known people who dabbled in this dangerous field and they have all disappeared. Yes, because they were ignorant fools who aroused within themselves forces as dark as those they were trying to manipulate and these forces simply annihilated them. Several times in the course of history whole continents have disappeared with all their inhabitants for no other reason than that they refused to acknowledge that higher forces and intelligences existed and that man must live in harmony with them.

And now, the Aquarian age is going to bring tremendous upheavals which will oblige the survivors to understand that there are laws which must be respected. The beauty, splendour and harmony of the new life that is being prepared is beyond imagination. All the creatures throughout the world who are secretly at work to bring about the Kingdom of God will unite and work together with such grandiose means that the strongholds of ignorance, materialism and despotism will crumble. This I am telling you and it will be so. Nothing will be strong enough to stand in the way of the new era, the Golden Age that has been foretold by many prophets, particularly by Nostradamus. This is why I say to all those who are unaware of these great truths: 'All of you who run after wealth and world domination so frantically, I warn you that, even if you succeed, you will never be satisfied. You are squandering all your most precious energies in pursuit of things that cannot last, that will disappear without a trace or, if they do leave a trace in the minds of men, it will be one of horror that will arouse the indignation and abhorrence of future generations.' Did Genghis Khan, Tamerlane, Attila, Nero, Hitler or Stalin leave traces of glory? No, their triumph was short-lived and soon forgotten.

It is time, now, to guide young people in a different direction. If I said that I knew pedagogical methods that exist nowhere on earth because they consist in starting the education of children even before they are born, all the educators in the world would be up in arms to prevent me from doing anything about it. I could give you proof of the efficacy of my method but I am prevented from doing so. For years and years, my application for French citizenship has been refused and, in this way, I am deprived of the means of helping your country to become the torch-bearer of humanity. Thousands of foreigners have been naturalized, but I have been refused. Of course, I know why: apparently even the C.I.A. suspected me of being a Soviet spy. Yes, but they have never been able to prove their suspicions.

And shall I tell you what I told an eminent jurist (a very nice, intelligent man) with whom I was discussing the situation? I said, 'It's true that I belong to the secret service of another country, but I know so many tricks that it is impossible to catch me out. In spite of all the inquiries and investigations that have been carried out, no one has ever been able to pin anything on me; that's because I'm much too wily, much too far-sighted and wary. I think we should tell those responsible for the security of France that they should come and take lessons from me and learn how I deal with cases of this kind.' He began to laugh because, of course, he understood that I was joking. Then I told him, 'But now I've started to write my memoirs and I want to talk about all my exploits as a spy. The trouble is, though, that I have a problem: I can't for the life of me remember the names of the people I have met or of the countries and towns I have been to. I can't even remember the dates. What a disaster to lose one's memory to such a degree!' 'I can tell already that your book is going to be a best-seller', he said, 'Everybody will read it'. And he began to laugh, too.

My dear brothers and sisters, Heaven has given me a philosophy that is capable of transforming every living creature on condition, of course, that they adopt it. And if there are people who want to do away with me − as, in the past, there have always been some who wanted to do away with those who brought something good, something just and divine to the world − they should remember that those who are massacred in this way always end by being glorified and sanctified. Even their ideas spread, for when they reincarnate, they have other powers and possibilities with which to continue the work that was interrupted. Whereas those who massacred them will also be eliminated... but they will be neither glorified nor sanctified. So, why do they persist in their ignorance of these sublime truths instead of working for a new order, for the one great family of the Universal White Brotherhood?

Izgrev, February 11, 1973

V

If you study the Hebrew letter Aleph א, you will see that it suggests a human figure with one arm raised to receive blessings from Heaven and the other reaching down to earth to distribute the gifts received. So, here again, we have a symbol which proves that we must be both capitalist and communist; a capitalist first, so as to be in a position, subsequently, to be a communist: first we must take and then we must give. As long as we continue to think of communism and capitalism as separate and contradictory, we are in error. A capitalist who only accumulates and never distributes anything begins to rot like wheat that is stored for years in a granary instead of being sown: it ends by being eaten by mice or going mouldy. The desire to have property of one's own is perfectly normal; but to want to possess things without ever giving anything to others is a primitive instinct that needs to be educated. What we possess must also be used to do good.

There is nothing wrong in wanting possessions. The only thing is, of course, that you must not restrict your desire to material wealth because, in order to become materially rich you are always obliged to dislodge a competitor or even defraud someone every now and then. The earth is limited and space is limited and, when we enrich ourselves, it is almost inevitable that it should be at someone else's expense. But if your desire for enrichment is focused on the vastness, the immensity, the infinity of Heaven, however much you acquire you can never diminish that immensity, that inexhaustible ocean; you will never be doing anyone down. And, once you are rich, you can distribute your wealth to others. One hand takes, therefore, and the other gives. This is how, like Christ, you become Aleph, you become perfect. Only when the two notions of capitalism and communism are joined can they really be resolved.

The ideal of an Initiate is to resemble Christ: Alpha and Omega, Aleph and Tav. Aleph and Tav, the beginning and the end, the cause and the consequences, the divine world and the physical world. Aleph sets in motion the forces of Heaven and Tav gives them concrete reality on earth. The same notion is seen in the *Solve et Coagula* of the alchemists: *Solve* is the process which dissolves matter and renders it etheric, and *Coagula* is the process that condenses matter. As a matter of fact, the name that I received in India, OMRAAM, corresponds to these two processes of *Solve* and *Coagula*. OM is that which dissolves and makes things subtler whereas RAAM materializes things and gives them concrete reality. The name OMRAAM, therefore, symbolizes a whole process of concretization: the invisible, intangible idea that has to become incarnate on earth so that all human beings may see and touch it. And we all have to work in this direction. So many people say, 'Oh, I have some fantastic ideas!' Yes, but what do they do to realize them? Nothing; they are content to have ideas.

When Jesus said, 'I am the Alpha and the Omega', he was saying, 'This is the tremendous philosophy that I am bringing you: to be linked to Heaven and draw down into oneself all Heaven's blessings so as to be able to project and materialize them here, on earth'. The same idea is expressed in another form in the Lord's Prayer: 'Thy will be done on earth as it is in Heaven'. The poor idealists who have nothing but their 'ideas' die of hunger; they are too sickly and weak. Their ideas may be excellent but they never achieve anything here, on earth. Whereas the rich are too often inwardly lifeless and rotten. Perfection demands both, therefore, and this is what we learn from the Teaching of the Universal White Brotherhood.

The solution to the problems of Capitalism and Communism depends on Capitalists and Communists agreeing to broaden their concepts and view things from a much higher level. Instead of fighting each other — which gets them nowhere — they must find some common ground, for they need each other. This is the solution I have found. There is no conflict in me between communists and capitalists, they both offer a friendly hand to the other, they embrace and are happy together. Night and day, the capitalists within me are busy getting rich; even the most ardent Capitalists on earth are limited and passive in comparison and don't work nearly so hard to get rich.

What can you do if you confine yourself to the earth? If you want to drive fast, you run the risk of colliding with all the houses and trees and people that get in your way. You often have to go at twenty miles an hour to avoid running over the chickens. Whereas, if you want to move about in the ether, even if you travel faster than light, there is no danger of a collision. And this is where my inner capitalists are, up on that level; that is why there is nothing to hinder them in their work. Whereas the wretched Capitalists on earth will always be limited, even if they do everything in their power to swallow up the whole world. What can you expect? That's how it is on earth. I'm a greater capitalist than any of them, and you cannot find fault with me for that. At the same time, since I realize that if I hoard my riches, they will go mouldy or be eaten by mice, I have also become a communist. Actually, we are all capitalists when we are born; it is only later that we become communists. When a young man falls in love with a girl, for instance, he becomes a communist. Yes, a family is the first community; that is where it all begins.

The wisest way, therefore, is to let both your capitalistic and communistic tendencies blossom. You should be able to be both in turn in the course of the same day. To be only a capitalist is to live in one's own little corner and have no awareness of anyone else, and that is very bad. On the other hand, to be always with other people because one is incapable of living alone, is a very dreary kind of communism. Personally, I have solved the problem by keeping half the day for myself. In that half I work and pray and meditate: I amass wealth. And the other half of the day is for others and I talk and receive people: I distribute my wealth. If you choose this way you will be happy because both aspects of your nature will be satisfied. If you are always alone and never give anything of yourself to others, you will feel unhappy and depressed; something will be lacking. If you are always with others, on the other hand, you will lose everything, your reservoirs will be drained dry and there will be nothing left for you. So you have to become a capitalist and spend a little less time with others and more time replenishing your wealth.

Both those who accumulate too much and those who distribute too much are unhappy. But I have found the third solution: half and half. This is the only solution that can make human beings happy. You think that all this is quite childish but, I assure you, it can have far-reaching repercussions. Take the case of married people, for instance: if they always share the same bed they are communists. Yes, but if they exaggerate their communism, they inevitably end by separating and rejecting each other, because there is no poetry left in their relationship. It is too prosaic to be always together in the same bed. If they really want to solve the problem, they are going to have to be a little more capitalistic, to be apart from time to time. It would be better if they sometimes had twin beds. What a lot of things in life are still not understood!

Only Initiates are genuine capitalists and genuine communists because they are fully conscious of being both. They know that the two currents must circulate, that it is a law of life, the law of give and take. Yes, this is eternal life: to receive gifts from Heaven so that we may distribute what we have received and that it may all be returned to Heaven, once again, to be purified. Our circulatory system is both capitalistic and communistic: the venous system is capitalistic because the blood from every part of the body collects in the lungs to be purified. And the arterial system is communistic because it sends the blood to the heart to be distributed throughout the body.

The circulation of the blood is a reflection of a cosmic process. The energy that comes from God, from the centre, flows through the different kingdoms of nature (human, animal and vegetable) to vivify them and, as it flows, it collects all kinds of impurities. Then, by ways which are still unknown to us, it returns to the lungs and heart of the universe to be purified and distributed, once again, to God's creatures. This, then, is the true meaning of capitalism and communism: this circulation. But the problem is that human beings are divided amongst themselves because they don't understand this meaning; that is why things are in such a sorry state. Communists must understand that Capitalists have a reason for existing and that they only need to be educated. They must tell them, 'You are truly magnificent, capable people! Heaven has given you great gifts, great will-power and great intuition. But you have become so submerged and over-burdened by your riches that you need to distribute them. And you must let us tell you where and how to do so because, so far, the results have not been very good.' Proof of this can be seen in the fact that no one is satisfied. The workers never stop complaining and making new demands and they will continue to be dissatisfied because they don't possess the light they need.

What is really behind this constant dissatisfaction? I'll tell you: it is that human beings, who have never understood that they must have a high ideal, a divine idea capable of renewing and purifying the atmosphere, end by being suffocated and poisoned. Whatever they do and wherever they go, even on holiday in the mountains or by the sea, they are always in a deplorable state of asphyxiation. Yes, even when they get away from their factories and workshops, they continue to suffer from a feeling of defeat because they have nothing to illuminate or purify them inwardly: they have lost contact with Heaven.

True communism is not a question of improving the material conditions of the workers. True communism is to be in communion with Heaven; this is the only way to be happy. Even if your work load is too heavy and conditions are poor, you will be able to put up with these difficulties and rise above conditions; nothing can really wear you down if you have something inside you that heals, enlightens and strengthens you. On the other hand, if you sever your ties with Heaven, no conditions, no material means will ever satisfy or console you, whatever you do; you will always have something to complain about.

To be sure, I'm not saying that there is anything magnificent about the life of workers or that there are not tremendous injustices that should be swept away for ever, but that is another matter. What I am saying is that if human beings continue to envisage the problem in the same old way, even if material conditions are greatly improved, they will continue to be plagued by the same discontent – or worse still – because, without the light, they will always have something to complain and be unhappy about. The mere fact that people are more and more angry and resentful in spite of the great improvements of recent years is proof enough of this. The only conclusion is that there is a lack of light, a lack of love, a lack of communion.

So, you see, it is the Communists who are not true communists because they are not in communion with Heaven; they only believe in material things: work, salary, the distribution of wealth. True communists are those who are in communion with Heaven and with human beings. The fact that the Communists have severed their ties with Heaven means that they will not last long. Their ambition is to propagate their philosophy throughout the world. At the moment, they are having considerable success and their success will continue for a few more years but, one day, it will all be over, for all men will understand, and then the new communism, the only genuine communism, that of the Universal

White Brotherhood, will reign in the world. It is good to be a communist, I am not against it but, as you see, there are still a few points that need to be cleared up.

Exactly sixty-one years ago, in 1917, I was seventeen years old. The Bolsheviks had just made their appearance and I remember saying to my mother, 'Communism will take over almost the whole world (since then it has even spread to Africa), but it will not be allowed to last very long; it will be transformed.' I have since read a similar prediction in a book about the seer, Edgar Cayce. Communism will not disappear, therefore; it will be transformed and blend into the spirit of brotherhood of our Teaching. Communists are brought up to accept notions of collectivity and brotherhood but, as long as they forbid the mystical and religious impulse to express itself, Communism cannot be the ideal solution. Even if their ideas are generous – and this is not always the case! – if the one essential element is missing, it cannot survive: men's souls and spirits will always demand the right to be in communion with the Lord. This means that there will be great upheavals in Russia for Russians are incapable of being atheists for long; they will explode! In this way, our Teaching will spread into Russia and Bulgaria and all the countries in which Communism has been in power for several decades. I hope that you will be alive to see the truth of what I say.

Let me give you another argument. Human beings all have certain desires, certain tendencies, lusts and appetites, but they know that they are not free to satisfy them in any way they like because there is a State, a government, laws and magistrates, and that if they break any of those laws, they will have to pay the penalty. It is no good saying, 'Oh, but I didn't know it was against the law to do thus and so!' You should have known. Ignorance is no excuse: everyone must know the law. Every civilized man knows that there are laws; even children know that if they break certain rules they will be punished with a slap or a beating.

Actually, if you are sufficiently cunning, it is possible to break certain human laws with impunity, but there are other laws which are above those of men, laws of a higher order, and no one can break them without being punished for it. These laws are not mentioned in human books; you have to learn about them in an Initiatic school or by studying them within yourself, for they are engraved within your being and we can all find them through reflection and meditation. These are the eternal laws of God. Human laws vary from one country to the next and from one period to the next and there are certain social advantages to be gained by respecting them but, as I have said, if you are sufficiently astute you can sometimes transgress them without being punished for it. The divine laws, on the other hand, are far mightier and more terrible, and it is essential to know them.

A disciple of the Universal White Brotherhood studies the divine laws and, to the extent to which he lives in harmony with them, he is sure to make progress. If he flouts them he will not be excused on the plea that it was not really his fault because he didn't know. He should have known. When a policeman arrests you, it's no good telling him that you didn't know you were breaking the law. He doesn't care twopence whether you knew or not: you still have to pay your fine. Why should it be any different in the spiritual domain?

Unfortunately, as people attach more and more importance to superficial things – gestures, their facial expressions, clothes and jobs – they are so busy studying what is socially acceptable that they have no time to study the divine laws. And this is why, as the material conditions of mankind improve, its moral and spiritual conditions deteriorate. Why is there so much illness? Why are so many people mentally disturbed? Why is there so much crime? If you knew all that goes on in the world every day: it's absolutely horrifying! Men have never been so well off on the material level but their physical and psychological ailments are increasing in geometric progression. And this is because, when you give absolute priority to one aspect, you inevitably let the other languish. People are always having meetings to discuss how to improve this or that, but they only talk about material things. They never come together to learn about the ways of God, and this is why they are so lost, even though business is flourishing.

An Initiate will tell you that anyone who doesn't study the divine laws is extraordinarily stupid because he is neglecting the relations that should exist between himself and all the creatures, entities and Hierarchies of the universe. He is confining himself to one little grain of sand, the earth, where the only thing that counts are his own petty concerns. There are so many things in the universe that people could know or with which they could communicate, but they turn their backs on them! This is why I say that communists and capitalists are much of a muchness. As long as both sides refuse to acknowledge that there are eternal laws to which they must conform and submit and with which they must harmonize themselves; as long as they continue to concentrate their energies exclusively on physical, material and economic questions, it means that their minds are obscured.

Become true capitalists and true communists and Heaven and earth will be yours. A lot of people are communists only under duress. Their land and house have been taken from them; it was not they who offered to give them away. It is a strange kind of communism that forces people to give up what belongs to them.

Is it communism to restrict and limit and crush others? No, communism is to give, to share, to love others and smile at them, but to keep one's capital assets for, if you give them away, they cannot earn anything. You may have plenty of ideas but, if you are penniless, you won't be able to put them into effect. Whereas if someone gives you some capital, you can start a business, earn a fortune and then distribute your wealth and, there you are: you're a communist! To be a true communist, then, you must first be a capitalist. What kind of communism can you practise if you possess nothing? Cosmic Intelligence has solved the problem for us: It has given us a capital of arms and legs, etc., and all the Capitalists who don't understand why they must be capitalists are very bad capitalists, and Communists have every reason to attack them. But they have no reason to attack the true capitalists of the Universal White Brotherhood, because they are also true communists.

You will say, 'My God! It's all too complicated; I'm in a complete muddle!' Yes, and everything will continue to be muddled in your head because you have not studied in an Initiatic school. You have studied goodness knows where, and now, when you hear an explanation of how Cosmic Intelligence has created things, you can't understand any of it. You have studied in purely human schools, stupid schools which have indoctrinated you with all kinds · of false ideas. But I have studied in the School of Cosmic Intelligence and this is what I learned: that if you are not a capitalist you cannot be a communist. So you must broaden your understanding, become a capitalist and use your wealth to do good with your brain, your mouth, your arms and legs, etc. Then you will be the perfect communist. But if you want to be a communist and have no capital, what good can you do? None! You will only be taking what doesn't belong to you. In other words, you will be a thief.

To do away with the rich in order to appropriate what is theirs and live as they live — is that how we should understand the question? When a man is destitute he is against the rich, but when he is rich himself they are no longer his enemies. Actually, it is when you are rich that you should be against the rich and distribute all your possessions. It is too easy to be against the rich when you are poor. You find the same thing amongst girls: plain girls criticize the pretty ones, because they know that they themselves are plain; if they were pretty they would never criticize beauty. I know human nature! Ugly girls speak ill of the beautiful ones who are attractive to boys because they have never attracted anyone. But, for my part, I am very broad-minded; I say, 'Well done! Attract as many as you can and bring them to the Brotherhood!' Believe me, I'm the most broad-minded man alive.

There, this is how you must look at things. You can't just say that you're a communist and believe that this gives you the right to plunder capitalists and oppress them even more viciously than those who have gone before you. How will Communists justify themselves in the eyes of history? Don't forget that everything is recorded. There are more and more films today that show how people are forced to confess to crimes they have never committed. Yes, but history will judge them; it will judge and condemn them all, Communists and Capitalists alike. Yes, all but those who are, at the same time, communists and capitalists, those who respect and protect their wealth – their purity, their life, their intelligence and light – so as to be able to distribute it to others and, in this way, achieve something great.

Yes, my dear brothers and sisters, everything else pales beside the Teaching of the Universal White Brotherhood. It is so vast, broad, noble, sublime and rich! No other system can hold a candle to it because no other system has ever given such comprehensive consideration to the true needs of human beings; and these are the needs of the soul and spirit, not only those with which Communism concerns itself. The Marxist system, therefore, will also turn out to be impoverished and incomplete – in fact, we can already see that it is bankrupt – and it is our Teaching that will have the last word.

Vidélinata (Switzerland), March 7, 1973

Chapter Five

True Economics

I

People are more and more inclined, nowadays, to give priority to the economic dimension and it seems, at first sight, that they are right to do so. It is obvious that if you haven't got enough money to pay for food and lodging things can be very complicated. But, in reality, the economy is not everything, for it depends on factors of a higher order. You might say that the economic aspect is the dead aspect: it cannot move or do anything by itself; it cannot express itself. There always have to be other elements that decide to move it from here to there and, depending on whether the decision is inspired by wisdom or by folly, the results will be totally different. When the head that decides on a move is ill, it is the economy itself that is wrecked. And then you have discontent, strikes and revolutions.

It is a pity that human beings have let themselves become so deeply immersed in matter that they forget that it is not matter that is the most important but the factors that influence it. Suppose that you have an immense amount of money and weapons and you feel very strong and secure. The only trouble is that you are also very stupid and, when someone who is more intelligent than you comes along, he can wipe you out, because he has an element at his command that is superior to everything you have. Yes, intelligence often triumphs over material means.

Every occurrence on the physical plane depends on phenomena that occur on a much higher plane, on the plane of thoughts and sentiments. I remember talking, one day, to somebody who held a very high position in the political sphere here in France, and he said that capital was the moving power behind society. But I replied, 'No. Just think for a moment: what moves capital from one place to another? Ideas. It is ideas that take precedence; it is ideas that control and displace capital, that fashion the world.' But human beings look no further than outward appearances. They see only the material aspects: capital, the lack or the abundance of raw materials, etc. They fail to see that all that is controlled and organized by human intelligence and will, which are spiritual elements. They seem to think that these are two separate worlds. As long as men fail to see the invisible element that influences and acts on the material dimension, whether for good or for evil, they will never understand reality. The truth is that nothing of an economic, technical or industrial nature can function all by itself.

When you want to describe the human body, you use a series of plates illustrating its different systems: the skeleton, the circulatory system, the muscles, the nervous system, etc. None of these plates represents the whole human being, only one aspect of the whole, and people do not realize that there are yet other systems still unknown to established science. For example, no one ever mentions the auric system with its currents of light and colour, and yet it is the auric system that controls the nervous system, just as the nervous system controls the circulatory, respiratory and other systems. Science has not yet studied every dimension of human beings.

Let's take an example from the field of medicine. One of the major landmarks in medical science was the discovery of the endocrine glands which secrete hormones. Nowadays, in fact, people believe that virtually everything depends on these glands, but this is not the case, for the fact that these glands sometimes secrete too much or too little means that they themselves are subject to other factors. Just as the endocrine glands influence the overall health of the organism, they in turn are influenced by other, subtler factors originating in a person's thoughts, emotions, soul or spirit. The day will come when medical science will study this question. It will also study the question of how the sun affects these glands.

By attaching prime importance to the economic dimension (raw materials, capital, commercial outlets, imports and exports and so on), human beings demonstrate that they have confined their attention to the three most material systems: the skeleton, the muscles and the blood. They have not got as far as the nervous system yet − not to mention the auric system! It is understandable that, when they focus all their energies on economic growth and on getting rich, it is to the detriment of certain rules, laws and virtues which correspond to the higher systems. This is why political leaders, who are principally concerned with the economy, are leading the whole of humanity to a state of decadence. If you are determined to be stronger and richer than your neighbour you will be obliged to do things which are not always perfectly honest. It is inevitable.

Whilst opulence is on the increase, therefore, respect for the divine laws is diminishing, and it is this that will lead to disaster for humanity. I know that people cannot accept what I am saying because they cannot see it. They are blind to the fact that to succeed on the economic level one is obliged continually to commit dishonest, criminal acts. It is the same in politics and espionage: anything goes! The excuse is that it is for the sake of one's country. Yes, but what about the other countries? When men are led to destroy moral principles it is always because their economic interests are at stake, and when you give these interests priority, all your noblest qualities are wiped out and replaced by egoism, violence and deceit and the complete absence of scruples. The economic dimension of life is certainly indispensable, I have no argument with that; but it must be kept under control and made to obey other necessities; other, higher powers. Otherwise man's highest aspirations will be trampled underfoot for the sake of a few egoists who want to be rich.

It is time men began to think about this and to understand clearly that it is the Divine World that must be given priority, and that everything else must be at its service. The fact is that human beings have mistaken the means for the end. They know that there is always a goal to be aimed at, and that there are various means for reaching that goal. What they don't see is that they are using all the most glorious faculties and talents that Heaven has given them as means in the pursuit of a terribly mundane, inglorious goal. They are ready to use their noblest qualities in order to gratify their basest appetites! They even expect the Lord Himself to aid and abet their licentiousness and their folly. And are they aware of all this? Not a bit of it! They never take the time to wonder what they are like or what they are looking for. No, it takes a spiritual Master to come and question them: 'Wait, my friend: look where you're going! Straight to Hell! And the means you are using? The Lord and His Angels, science, art and religion... Yes, you are using all these things to help you along the road to Hell!'

Material, economic life is the only thing that counts for most people and they are so ignorant and underdeveloped on the higher planes, that they are constantly anxious and ill without understanding the reason. Then, of course, they put the blame on others – the neighbours, society, the government and the Lord Himself. They don't understand that their problems come from a lack in themselves, that they haven't got the ability to see things clearly nor the strength and goodwill to remedy the situation. Oh, no; it is always other people who are to blame for not having given them this or that. The truth is that, even if they were given what they demand, nothing much would change because, when someone is too stupid and inwardly limited, he is incapable of taking advantage of what he is given: instead of getting better, he gets worse.

We have often seen that a man doesn't become nobler and

more radiant or more divine when his desires are all satisfied; on the contrary, he becomes more and more of an animal because he has more possibilities for self-degradation. Poverty at least kept a rein on his appetites! But as soon as he succeeds in improving his material circumstances, the road to Hell lies open before him. I am not saying that men must be held down in a state of poverty; not at all. What I am saying is that it is dangerous to give material facilities to those who have never learned self-control and who attach more importance to the material than to the spiritual life, for this only encourages them in habits of sloth, weakness and crime.

An Initiate who already knows where the gratification of this or that desire would lead him, what it would arouse in him and the lengths to which it could drive him, refuses to indulge his desires if he sees that they would be an obstacle to his spiritual advancement. Let's take an example from everyday life: an ignorant, spineless young man falls in love and marries a girl who is ravishingly beautiful. At first sight this is magnificent, but as he has never worked to cultivate his powers of comprehension, self-control or nobility of character, all his baser instincts – suspicion, jealousy and cruelty – begin to get the upper hand and he never knows a minute's peace. He is forever watching his wife and anyone who comes near her; he is convinced that she is being unfaithful to him, and one day, in a fit of jealous rage, he murders her and the man he suspects of being her lover, and lands in prison. Socrates was much wiser: he looked for the ugliest and most disagreeable woman in Greece because he knew that he wouldn't have anything to worry about. From time to time, of course, he had to put up with some domestic storms, when she screamed at him or threw a bucket of dirty water on his head, but all that was purely external. Inwardly, he was at peace. But would any of you choose to marry a Xanthippe? Oh no; you'd rather marry a beauty queen and suffer torments all your life.

So, once again, I repeat: if you don't understand human nature and are bent on giving people what they ask for, the Lord knows whether it will be for their good or whether you are not preparing coals of fire that will pour down on their heads! Why not educate human beings, instead, and teach them to analyse what they are seeking and demanding so as to see whether it is really what is best and most constructive for them? Time and again, things that seemed, at first, to constitute a step forward, an advantage or improvement, have turned out to be extremely damaging... all because everybody relied on first appearances.

It is true that material and industrial progress makes a positive contribution to life. It is amazing how many appliances people have in their homes: heating systems, vacuum cleaners, washing machines and dish washers, televisions, telephones, etc. But why, when they have got everything, are human beings more discontented, rebellious and unhealthy than ever? What is even more astonishing is that, in spite of this obvious failure, people still continue to look for happiness in the same direction. They refuse to understand that, if they want to be happy, they must seek something quite different. They must seek love, wisdom and truth and be a little less sure that gadgets and comfort will give them all they want. The only things an easy, comfortable life can give you are sloth, selfishness and weakness; and the sad thing is that this is what people want: idleness and pleasure; to do nothing and have everything!

And what do I advise? I advise you to have both: have all the material facilities you want and, at the same time, keep working, night and day, so as to avoid becoming stiff in mind and body. You will say that I have already talked to you about this. That is true; I have. But has it done any good? Have you made up your minds to act on my advice? No, not yet. You, too, are so preoccupied by material things and by your pleasures that you have no time to open your hearts to the divine world and ask for sublime entities to come and work within you. This is very serious, very regrettable: if you refuse to understand you will have to suffer, and no one will be able to save you. Only you can save yourself by means of light and love. Analyse the use you make of your time and energy, therefore, and ask yourself what occupies the bulk of your attention. You will see that the divine world does not take up much room in your life — although this is the only thing capable of purifying, enlightening and resuscitating you — and that you devote almost all your time and energy to the material world which can only give you a few moments of joy before becoming a burden, a prison, an instrument of destruction.

In a previous lecture I told you that human beings were inhabited by two forces, two contradictory tendencies which I represented to you as the two symbols, Erebus and Ionah. In Genesis, Erebus is the crow and Ionah the dove sent out by Noah to see if the waters of the Flood had subsided. These two forces — the forces of inertia and motion, of expansion and contraction, of life and death — are in constant conflict within man, and depending on which force gains the upper hand, man is either active, dynamic and strong, or weak, spineless and irresolute. Ionah manifests itself principally during the periods of childhood, adolescence and adulthood. When it begins to diminish, Erebus begins to manifest itself and man gradually weakens and dies.

If men knew the law of love, wisdom and truth, if they kept in close contact with Heaven, they would be able to encourage and sustain Ionah even when its strength begins to be limited by opposing forces. But human beings are so estranged from spiritual realities that, even from a very early age, they reinforce the influence of Erebus within them. At eighteen or twenty, they're already old and decrepit, their vigour undermined by the inferior thoughts and feelings that they continually entertain. Human beings want to stay young, they are always looking for ways to prolong their life, but they don't know how to set about it: they take pills or get injections of glandular extracts, but these methods are not effective.

The most effective methods are spiritual. I have seen this time and again. Only the day before yesterday, a very old woman came and listened to my lecture: to start with, her face was sad and without light but, gradually, as she listened, a light began to glow and intensify within her until she was completely transformed. How can anyone fail to recognize that the spiritual life is capable of transforming human beings? I know that you have all seen such things, too. This means that you must try to give more and more encouragement to good thoughts and feelings and good impulses within yourself, because their effects are extremely beneficial not only for your psychic life but also on the physical plane. In other words, if man lives a truly spiritual life in light, love and peace, he can prolong the life of Ionah.

Of course, however great your knowledge and goodwill, you cannot expect to be totally transformed in this incarnation: the progress a human being can hope to accomplish in his lifetime is more or less determined before birth. So, although it is possible to improve to a certain extent in this life, any really substantial improvements will take effect only in your next incarnation. In your next incarnation, Heaven will take into account all the good intentions and desires you have today and, overlooking what you were in the past, will grant you a magnificent destiny. Your present life reflects your past incarnations. Depending on the life you had led previously, the Twenty-Four Elders decreed the kind of body and the kind of physical and intellectual capacities you should have. Today, thanks to the purer and more harmonious life you are living in the Teaching, and thanks to your prayer and meditations, you can improve a certain number of things, but it is very difficult to remedy everything. You can do everything for the future, but not for the present.

The advantage of being a member of the Universal White Brotherhood is that it gives you the conditions you need to make your future incarnations brighter. Without this, not only would you fail to improve anything, but your situation might well go from bad to worse; your health might be even worse and you might be even poorer and more limited next time. Take the example of someone who is very rich: if he doesn't use his money to do good, if he is content to enjoy the pleasures of a mediocre way of life, in his next incarnation he will be a penniless tramp and spend his days drinking with his fellow tramps. He will not even know that he was once very rich and is poor today because he didn't use his money to do anything for anyone else. So many human beings come into the world in a truly woeful state and never know why. Neither psychology nor medical science, neither psychoanalysis nor the science of education – nor even religion – has ever shed much light on this question. Only Initiatic Science is capable of shedding any light on the question.

It sometimes happens, therefore, that the emanations and radiations of our psychic life manifest their effects even on the physical plane and, if only for a few moments, a man can be truly transfigured. He soon resumes his normal appearance but, if he works consciously to renew and revive these marvellous states, he will be building a body of indescribable splendour for his next incarnation. Before you undertake anything, therefore, whatever it may be, begin by saying to yourself, 'I am looking for light; I'm looking for love and strength. Shall I find them if I do this?' and, thanks to this Initiatic Science, you will immediately be given the answer. Otherwise, you will plunge headlong into activities that will end by killing you. You will be like all those tycoons who want to be king of the oil or steel or any other industry: many of them fall ill or end by committing suicide. The weight of their responsibilities and the excessive amount of work they do in the attempt to satisfy their greed and their obsessive need to swallow up the whole world end by destroying them. Their nervous system cannot support the strain: they get insomnia, ruin their health and lose all their zest for life. Before setting out to possess the world, you must study every angle of the situation and see what the consequences will be.

I know very well that no one will accept or understand or be guided by what I say in this area, either. People know what they know! They cling to their pet ambitions and lusts, and there is nothing anyone can do about it. Who will agree with me? All the paupers of this world; all those who are poor and idle. Yes,

they will be on my side, but will they have understood what I
am saying? Just try giving them some material advantages, try
improving their lot and you will soon see whether they have
understood or not! They will go to even greater lengths of folly
and wickedness than the others. If poor people are always curs-
ing the rich, it is because they want to be rich too, and as they
are not, all they can do is rail against those who are. But give
them some money and you will see. Do I speak disparagingly of
the rich? Never. I speak out against their lack of understanding,
that's true; but I love the rich. I love them so much, in fact, that
if they gave me all their millions for the embellishment of the
Brotherhood, I would hug them with all my heart! Well, however
that may be... never trust people who are always denigrating someone: it means that they would like to have what he has or to do
what he does. Yes, my analysis is terrible. Never lay yourselves
open to my analysis.

There is still much to say about this question of economy!
When a society is too preoccupied by its economic interests, it
leads to an imbalance in the life of the community and all kinds
of difficulties which, with a little wisdom, might have been fore-
seen. Suppose a country wants to export as much as possible
because it is extremely profitable to do so: one thing leads to
another and, before long, they are selling arms and fighter planes
to countries whose constant wars endanger the peace and safety
of the entire planet. The people in some of these countries can
barely read and write and yet they are allowed to buy the most
sophisticated weaponry! Of course, that is one way to earn a lot
of money, but the price to be paid in other ways will be exorbit-
ant. In God's name, how can people be so blind? This is just
one example of how economics can spell ruin for many countries.

Yes, my dear brothers and sisters, I fully agree that nothing is
more important than the economy. But there is one thing that human beings have failed to understand, and that is that if they want
to solve the problem they must study it in the world above and not
below, for what is below is only a reflection of what is above.

Nature alone really understands economics; only she knows how things must be organized so that not a single atom is lost. Every speck of dust, every scrap of refuse is utilised. Look what happens to all the rubbish and detritus that is thrown away by human beings: the earth absorbs it and sends it down to its underground factories to be recycled and transformed into food for the vegetation on the surface. Nothing is wasted; nothing is discarded. But human beings, who are so out of touch with the intelligence of the earth, are constantly plagued by the question of wastes. Look at the problems caused by the disposal of radioactive and other toxic wastes which cannot be destroyed! They have to be stored away underground but they constitute a terrible threat to mankind.

What understanding of economics can anyone have if he inwardly vandalizes everything, if he squanders and dissipates everything because of his passions and desires and his disordered thoughts and feelings? You will tell me that you don't see any connection. But of course there is a connection; these are not two separate, disconnected realms. And this is why those who are responsible for the economy of a country must not decide the issues on the physical plane before they have learned the essentials: how man is designed and put together; how he is linked to the universe; how the universe is hierarchically organized, and how all human organization must adhere to a divine model, a Heavenly idea. They won't find any of these things in books about economics, but once they understand them, all that they do and all the decisions they make will be perfect.

Vidélinata (Switzerland), March 17, 1974

II

Human beings are so designed that they always count on the support of someone or something. A woman counts on her husband, a man counts on his wife, children count on their parents. Also, everybody counts on money, circumstances, the weather, and so on. In itself, this is not bad, but what is bad is that people have got into the habit of always counting on something external. Are you ill? There are plenty of doctors and pharmacists. Are you ignorant? You can always ask a professor – or a clairvoyant – to tell you the future. Have you damaged your car? There are plenty of repair shops. Are you bored? There are cinemas, bars, night clubs for your entertainment, etc., etc.

Life is so well organized to provide human beings with whatever they need that they have become very negligent: they know that they can always find something or somebody to get them out of a fix. They can go skiing and risk their lives on the slopes: if they break a leg they can always go to hospital and get a plaster cast. If they are working at the top of a ladder, why bother to make sure that it can't slip: if they fall off, someone will pick them up and take care of them. Why take care of their teeth? Dentists are there for that. Why be careful not to stain their clothes? There are so many cleaning fluids on the market these days! And, if they go for a walk in the forest and throw

away a lighted cigarette, why get all upset if it starts a forest fire?
The firemen will come and put it out!

Because of this attitude, people's powers of attention and their
perspicacity, dexterity, wisdom and intelligence are constantly
diminishing. They see no reason to cultivate these qualities when
society offers so many ways of remedying their mistakes. Technicians and researchers are all working to help humanity, but the
fact of the matter is that they are not helping, for people are losing their personal initiative and becoming steadily lazier and less
capable of doing things for themselves. They probably know more
than they used to, but they are also much more careless and
lackadaisical. I am not saying that we should put a stop to material
progress; what I am saying is that we should also continue to
work inwardly so as to grow in attentiveness, prudence and self-
control. Because, if you break or dent something, for instance,
even though there are ways of repairing the damage, it will always
bear the mark; it will never be perfect again. How much better
it would be not to break it in the first place!

Then, too, we have to remember that there is always a
possibility of events occurring that would deprive us of all our
comforts and facilities. Look at what happened with world supplies of oil, for instance: only a few years ago it was produced
and consumed and wasted without restraint because people
thought that it would always be there for the asking. And now?
Progress is wonderful; it makes life so much easier! Believe me,
I am not against progress; on the contrary. In fact, I could mention several things that nobody has any suspicion of today and
that science will discover in the future. But, for the time being,
the most important thing for you is to know and accept the truths
that are capable of transforming you and to improve your inner
life before improving your external circumstances.

Initiatic Science tells us that, however great the benefits that
come from outside ourselves, they will never fulfil us, for fulfilment can only be found in one's own efforts, in efforts of the
will, the intelligence and the imagination. In any case, you all

know this: you all know that you find real satisfaction only in what you achieve for yourselves; you can never get the same joy and happiness from externals that are acquired without effort, even money. Yes, everyone knows this and yet everyone continues to look outside themselves for what they need. This is why their problems are never solved. However much you possess, however much other people give you, you must never abandon your own inner work; keep working until the very last minute.

No, I'm not against progress, but material progress is not true progress. Material progress is certainly to be encouraged but you must never rely on it. See it as something magnificent, as something that opens up immense possibilities, but don't look to it for satisfaction. Look for satisfaction only from your work. What work? The only true work: spiritual work.

So, as I say, it is fantastic to have so many tools and products to remedy our accidents and mistakes; nowadays, everything can be patched up, glued together, cleaned or mended. But the trouble is that nobody attaches any importance to the other aspect, to the care and attention that would lead to less breakages. No, nobody bothers about that; why should they? As I have said, the pharmacies, hospitals, garages, laundries and dry cleaners are there to remedy all the accidents and mistakes committed by human beings. Mankind continues to make progress in external things, therefore, but the situation on the inner level is deplorable. And then people talk about the economy!

True economy is to use things with care and reason; anything else is wasteful. Do young people know anything about economy? They squander all their strength and energy in mad schemes and the pursuit of sensations, and that is anything but economical. I am, perhaps, the only person in the world who understands economics correctly. People discuss the economy and study economic science and I know nothing of all that; but I do know that economy is not what people think it is. Do you want to practise true economics? Do you want to be very rich, to acquire a fortune in order to help others? In that case you must become more attentive, enlightened and reasonable; you must learn self-mastery. This is the only true economics. But no one expects to find economics in these things, and the most extravagant and ruinous spending is caused by economists because they have never studied true economics.

People are in the process of ruining themselves spiritually, morally, intellectually and even materially, because no one understands the true nature of economics. Let me give you an example: suppose you are talking to your boss or a business associate and, through carelessness, you say something that makes him very angry. All because of a lack of attention you are dismissed or your associate breaks off relations, and you find yourself with all kinds of legal and financial problems. You say that you can sort things out again; that may be true but, even then, it will involve a lot of trouble and expense. So, one day, you are going to have to understand that you must be very careful and very reasonable so as not to complicate things, at least within yourself. There will always be disorder and conflict on the external level and there's not much you can do about it. It is not so easy to restore order in the world. But you can make sure that harmony, order, peace and light prevail in all that you yourself do.

If you work in this way for years, you will see the results: all your problems will sort themselves out, even on the material plane, because everyone will like and respect you and be eager to render you service and help you. Yes, all your economic problems can be solved if you apply a little wisdom. If you really want to live a magnificent life you must make up your mind today and begin at once to be more attentive. Of course, it would be better for some of you if you had started sooner because it is when you are still young that what you do and say must be marvellous and harmonious and beneficial. That is true economics!

Castelrama, November 23, 1975

III

Human beings have invented all kinds of conveniences to give themselves the favourable conditions they need in order to cultivate their faculties and talents, but there is one point that they have consistently overlooked, and that is the question of attention.

There are several different kinds of attention. The kind that is most familiar to us is the deep and sustained mental application we need in order to do our work properly, listen to a lecture or read a book. But there is another kind of attention, which we can call self-observation, consciousness or analysis, and which consists in being aware, at every moment of the day – and even of the night – of what is going on within oneself, of the currents, desires and thoughts that go through one and of the influences and impulses that move one. It is this kind of attention that is still not sufficiently developed. It is easy to pay attention to one's physical gestures; anyone who works in a factory or a laboratory learns to do so, otherwise he might well lose a hand or a leg. But the kind of inner attention and vigilance advocated by the Initiates is almost unknown, and this lack is often at the origin of much suffering and many accidents and mishaps: people are unaware of what is going on within them.

The Gospels tell us, 'Be vigilant, because your adversary the devil walks about like a roaring lion, seeking whom he may devour.' Don't worry! You will meet neither lion nor Devil on the physical plane; the danger is lying in wait for you in your inner life. That is where all kinds of lusts, desires, ambitions and passions prowl about and, if you are neither enlightened nor vigilant, they will devour you. Why do parents never think of fostering vigilance in their children? They should start to do so even when they are very young, for this lack of self-observation and analysis, this inattention to what goes on in one's inner sanctum is at the root of a great deal of suffering.

This is why I tell you that the beginning of true economics is somewhere where you have never thought to look for it: in attention. It is staggering to see the number of means and products that exist to mend or renovate things that have been damaged, broken or stained — and not only inanimate objects, but human beings as well. It's amazing: one half of the world population works at repairing the damage done by the other half. Well, this is something that economists should give more thought to, the fact that people rely too much on external means and tell themselves, 'Why bother to take care when there are so many technicians and workers capable of mending whatever I break, including myself?' The more conveniences people have the less they develop the faculty of attention, and this is what destroys an economy: too much has to be spent on repairs.

Of course, I know very well that this is not the economists' point of view. Not only have they never envisaged the problem in this way, but their philosophy is diametrically opposed. They say that we must produce more and more goods and, in order to keep stocks rolling, people must buy as much as possible. They urge people to consume, therefore, and not only to consume but to waste. The more goods they buy the better it will be. If they are careless and wreck their car or break a major appliance in their home, so much the better: they will have to buy new ones. If they live irresponsibly and ruin their health, that, too, is all to the good: they will be contributing to a thriving pharmaceutical industry. Naturally, in this way, the commercial and financial affairs of cer-

tain individuals and countries will prosper but, for mankind as
a whole, for its physical and psychological health and well-being,
this conception of economics is ruinous, catastrophic.

True economics, therefore, will not be found where most
people look for it. True economics consists, in fact, in *not* wasting,
in not wasting the forces, qualities and energies that Heaven has
given us. True economics begins with wisdom, moderation and
attention. There are swarms of economists in the world today;
impossible to get away from them! But mankind will never find
happiness by following their philosophy because they see nothing
but the material aspect of life and its problems.

First and foremost, economics must begin on a higher level, the
level of intelligence, in the thoughts, words and looks of human
beings, in the way they live and behave. For it is not enough to
avoid falling and injuring oneself or breaking something; you
must also avoid transgressing the laws of the invisible world. It often happens that, without in the least realizing it, a person triggers
certain mechanisms, disturbs certain entities or breaks certain laws
on the psychic plane and, when this happens, he has to suffer the
consequences and pay the penalty. One sometimes meets people
who are always very attentive on the physical plane and yet they
fall ill. This is because, through their thoughts, feelings or desires,
they have triggered a reaction from hostile forces. And now they
are in bed and are going to have to spend a lot of time and money
to be cured. There are a lot of people who are considered to be
first-rate economists. They may be first-rate in the theory of economics, yes; but just look at how they live! Look at all the excesses they indulge in, at all the waste in their lives. From the point
of view of Initiatic Science, economics begins with the way we live.

This is what I want to emphasize, therefore, the necessity for
this inner attention, this constant awareness that allows you to see
what is going on within yourself at every moment of the day or
night and to recognize the currents and influences that pass
through you. Personally, I have practised this wakefulness for so
long that I know exactly what is going on within me at any given

moment. I have trained myself to become fully conscious and, as I can recognize the origin and nature of every idea, thought or feeling, I am in a position to take the necessary precautions. You must learn to be attentive. I have often asked someone, 'What are you thinking about?' and heard the reply, 'I don't know'. He doesn't know because he has never looked into himself, and that means that any currents, any filth, any mental images, however frightful, are free to come and go at leisure and he won't even notice. How can he hope to create a glorious future for himself in these conditions? It is possible to use your thoughts to create the future, but not if you are so utterly inattentive and unconscious. This is why children should begin their education by learning to be attentive. In every family, school and university, young people must be taught to be attentive.

As for you, the very first quality that you must acquire, now that you are in the Brotherhood, is the quality of attention. Why do you think I have tried to get you into the habit of eating in silence, without making a noise with your knives and forks (seven hundred people eating together and not a sound to be heard!)? In order to help you to cultivate this faculty of vigilance; in order to teach you to control every single gesture, to use your knife and fork and cut up your food without making a sound.

If you want to acquire self-mastery, begin by practising at meals. If you can learn to move all the objects on the table without knocking them against each other, you will find that this harmony will be reflected in everything you do during the rest of the day. Yes, simply because you practised while you were eating! Then, not only will you make the effort not to make a noise, but you will begin to focus your attention on your food. From the first mouthful you will be filled with wonder: what strength, what energy and vitality God has put into that mouthful of food! If you can learn to eat in this state of attention and harmony, you will be capable of undertaking all kinds of activities, all day long, without getting tired.

The Bonfin, July 28, 1978

IV

Once again, this evening, we find ourselves in the presence of one of life's greatest mysteries: fire. Why do I say that it is one of the greatest mysteries? Fire shows us that, without sacrifice, life cannot go on. When you light a fire, all the black, twisted branches start to burn and are transformed into energy, light and heat. This is why you must make up your minds to light a fire within yourselves, so as to burn up all your refuse and transform it into light and warmth. As long as you think of sacrifice as a deprivation, an impoverishment, it means that you haven't understood the first thing about it. True sacrifice is a transformation of old, worn out, impure elements into light and heat, that is to say, into love and wisdom. For heat is simply divine love and light is divine wisdom.

This evening you must ask the Angel of Fire to come and burn up all the rubbish and all the old, ugly things accumulated within you, and transform them into love and wisdom. He is perfectly capable of doing it. Of all the four elements, fire is the most powerful. To be sure, earth, water and air are also powerful, but less so than fire: nothing can stand up to fire. And the divine fire, the sacred fire of God will soon burn up all the enemies of the Kingdom of God, all the enemies of light, the enemies of the Universal White Brotherhood. This has already been decreed and, sooner or later, you will witness it: they will all be consumed by fire, exterminated, wiped out, because the Kingdom of God must be established on earth.

Actually, as we are told by Holy Scripture, the battle will not be between men but between spirits: the good spirits will wage war against the evil spirits. The enemies we have to fight are not men but the influences and entities that dwell in men and combat the light. The instant a man is released from the hold of these spirits he changes. It is not rival armies of human beings, therefore, that will combat each other, but influences, forces and currents. This is the war of the future and, as foretold in the Apocalypse, the Dragon, the collective symbol of all the disorders and hatreds of mankind, will be defeated.

As you watch this fire and see how beautiful and powerful it is, ask it to come and burn in your hearts and souls. It is not dangerous. It will not destroy you; on the contrary, it will vivify you. I have already talked to you about the different sorts of fire: subterranean fire, physical fire, the fire of Hell, etc. Also the fire of the stars and the sun's fire, the truest, purest and most vivifying fire of all; that which we try to attract and invite into us every morning at sunrise. The aura is also a fire, a fire which, if it is sufficiently powerful and bright, protects a person from evil spirits. Not all human beings have an aura capable of protecting them; it is often too weak and dull and, in this case, all kinds of noxious beings and elements can slip through it. The aura of the great Initiates, on the other hand, can be several miles wide and has the power to console, sooth, encourage, enlighten and heal.

And now, let's concentrate on the fire and send it a great deal of love and a great deal of respect and veneration. The fire is alive. It knows us; it knows who we are and the degree of evolution we have reached. If you knew how to consult it, it could enlighten you about many things.

Before beginning their ceremonies, Magi and Initiates light

candles or lamps. This tradition comes from a very ancient science which taught that fire was indispensable to realization. A remnant of the same tradition continues in the practice of lighting candles in church. This is why I asked you to write down your requests and give them to the Angel of Fire. All those little pieces of paper have been burned but your prayers have been transcribed and recorded on high by the servants of the Angel of Fire. If you are capable of working in accordance with the wishes expressed in your prayers, they will be granted for, when fire has a hand in anything, the results are always outstanding. When you are assailed by certain inner difficulties, if you have a sensation of sadness or distress, for instance, or if you are discouraged or sorely tempted, write down a prayer for strength and peace of mind, light a candle and ask the Angel of Fire to consume your distress in his fire, and he will do so. When you don't know about this sacred Science, you have to drag yourselves through life, unable to break out of the vicious circle of distress and tears. Fire is there to help us but, apart from the Initiates, who ever thinks of using it in their spiritual life?

Now that it is time for you to go home you must take care to hold on to the warmth, the sacred fire, that you have received here. People are rarely conscious of these things: when you go home after spending several weeks here, you don't think about protecting all this warmth and light, this fire, which is basic to all true spiritual evolution and fulfilment. From now on, remember to preserve this heat, to keep it alive for a long time in your heart and soul. This is true economy: to preserve the heart's warmth, to economize it so that it not only stays within you for a long time, for the rest of your life, but so that it grows and is amplified. You know how to economize money, material objects or time, but you don't know how to economize the one thing that is vital, this warmth. No, I'm afraid you are still a long way off! Within a few days you will have dissipated all this warmth and will be shivering with cold again. If you know how to look at fire, if you know what thoughts and what love you should have as you look at it, it will reveal the greatest mysteries to you: how to preserve the warmth and light you have received.

Let's stay here for a few more minutes and meditate on true economics.

The Bonfin, October 1, 1978

Chapter Six

Wealth

I

Money is not, as many people believe, 'the root of all evil'. There is something within human beings that uses money as a means to express its greed. Do away with money and put anything else in its place and, as long as people continue to be possessed by their own weaknesses, base appetites and passions the problem will be the same. So it is not money that is to blame, but man. Man is not sufficiently enlightened, he doesn't know what attitude to adopt with regard to money, how to use it properly, for what reasons and what purpose it should be used. In itself, money is neither good nor bad; it is neutral. At the same time, it is a tremendously powerful means in the hands of those who possess it and this is why it can be used either to destroy or to save. The whole question, therefore, is one of attitude. Money is powerful simply because human beings attribute great value to it. If they decided, tomorrow, to divest money of its value and attribute it to something else, the same pattern would repeat itself all over again, with the same tragedies, the same seductions, the same splendours and the same degradations.

As long as money has value and that value allows men to satisfy their appetites, they will continue to concentrate on it as a means of obtaining all they need or desire; it is only normal. But it still remains that they must have the right attitude towards it. As I have often told you: keep your money in your safe or in your pocket, but never in your head. If you keep it in your head it will be an opaque screen that will cloud your vision. If you keep it before your eyes as an ideal to be reached at all costs, the evil counsel it gives you will be your downfall. You will be less ready to see people's good points; you will be less considerate, generous and tolerant. You will become severe, intransigent and cruel. To have no money at all, on the other hand, is not desirable either. People have sometimes wanted to live in stark poverty, thinking that it would enhance their spiritual life, and have ended by becoming a useless burden to society. That is not the ideal solution! As long as we are on earth and things are organized as they are today, we need money.

Perhaps, in the future, there will be no more money: our currency will be love. Yes, why not? Love is a far more valuable currency than gold! But it is still too soon for mankind to achieve this conception of things and, as we may be sure that money will be with us for some time to come, it is important to have the right ideas about it so as to avoid becoming a prey to its seductive wiles. That is all we need: the right attitude. It is not wrong to have money. How could you help others if you had no money? It is all very well to have a heart full of love but, if you have nothing else, you still cannot help people materially. I seem to be talking to you as though I had to persuade you — as though you needed to be persuaded that money was necessary! I know that I don't have to worry about that: you all agree that we need money. The only question is how to behave where money is concerned, how to use it.

If you give money to someone who has not achieved the mastery of his thoughts, feelings and desires, he will hasten to use it and abuse it for his own debasement. His new wealth will enable him to ruin his enemies, have all the women he wants, etc. You cannot pin the blame on the money: it is simply a means to satisfy his desires; if the desires of his heart are evil, it is not the fault of money. You can say the same for anything else: oil, gas, coal etc.: you can use them all for constructive or destructive purposes and, if you choose to use them for an evil purpose, it is not their fault. The fault lies with you who harbour evil in your heart.

The conclusion to be drawn from all this is that you must first transform yourself so as to be capable of using money and all your other possessions for no other purpose than your own elevation and the good of humanity. Once you achieve this, you can possess billions and still not fall a prey to it, still resist its lures; you will be in a position, then, to realize the sublime things that you have dreamed of for so long.

Those who are still weak, still subject to their passions should not be given money; that is clear, but if you give money to Masters and Initiates, they will never use it for anything but good. So it is human beings who need to be changed for the better and money can be left to fulfil the purpose for which it was meant; it is not at fault. I have so often heard people saying, 'Money is the cause of all our misfortunes'. Well, they say that as long as they haven't got any, but as soon as they get some we hear a different tune. In the first place, therefore, they are being stupid in failing to recognize the true cause of their misfortunes and, in the second place, they are being dishonest. Two terrible failings! What they should say is, 'Money is very, very necessary. In fact, it's wonderful; but Heaven forbid that I should ever become a slave to it!'

If you think that money is the only thing that matters, you will end by sacrificing all your best and most beautiful qualities to it. In fact, by the time you have all the money you want, you will have effectively destroyed the very qualities that would have enabled you to savour the pleasures and delights that wealth can buy. This is the danger: you will have everything you have ever desired and still be unhappy because you will have destroyed the element that enabled you to find such exquisite, subtle flavour in every experience. This is the greatest misfortune: to be in a position to have everything you want, to indulge all your desires and to be incapable of enjoying or getting any pleasure out of any of it.

Of course, it is also terrible to be destitute and penniless. But if you had the choice between possessing everything and being incapable of enjoying it on the one hand and, on the other, of possessing nothing but of preserving your powers of enjoyment, you would be better off with the second alternative for, when you have a sense of taste, you can delight in whatever comes your way. If you had to choose, you should always choose to keep this power of enjoyment for it is also linked to health. To be sure, the best of all is to have both: money and the ability to enjoy it. If I see someone hurrying to give me money, I'm not going to fly into a rage and refuse it, but I have not devoted my life to trying to get a lot of money. If it comes, as I say, I'm not going to refuse it or drive it away, but I would never abandon my work to go in search of it: never!

To retain your ability for enjoyment, that is what counts. But only light can give you this sense of taste, this capacity to enjoy everything. Once you have found the light, whatever your activities, whether you are eating, working or going for a walk, everything has the most delicious flavour.

If you don't work with light, if you don't understand what light is, it means that you have not understood the first thing about life. Light is all: light created the world; light is the cause of the universe. Light is a spirit, a spirit that comes from the sun. Each ray is a tremendous force which travels throughout the universe to penetrate matter and accomplish its work in it. If ever there were a subject that needed to be studied in depth it is the subject of light: the nature of light, how it works and how we can use it and work with it. He who abandons light and focuses exclusively on money and his business interests is on the wrong track for the gold he is pursuing is, in fact, simply a condensed form of light. Yes, gold is a condensation of the sun's rays which have been collected and fashioned by creatures living underground. What happens when you put gold and silver on a pedestal and neglect light? It means that you are forgetting the father, the cause of all things. Or, if you prefer, you are neglecting the lady of the manor and paying court to her servant. Naturally enough, when her mistress sees this, she will close her door to you and tell you, 'It is I who am entitled to the place of honour; I see you courting my cook or my chambermaid whereas you should be giving first place in your love and respect to me. Very well, all doors will be closed to you!'

When you have money it opens all doors in the physical world, that is true. But the other doors, the doors of peace, happiness, joy and inspiration, the doors of all the qualities and virtues remain closed to you. What good will it do you to find all other doors open if the doors of the sanctuary remain closed to you? Are you incapable of feeling joy or of taking pleasure in anything you do? It is a sure sign that the spiritual doors are closed to you and this means that you have a wrong understanding of life and the values of life.

You must give your love and homage to the lady of the house, the princess; in this way her servants will also serve you. The princess will tell them, 'Give him food and drink; give him clothes and a room', and her servants will hasten to obey: 'Yes, my lady; yes, Your Highness.' Gold is the servant whom we cherish so dearly that we never think about whose service she is in. Gold is dependent on the light of the sun; it is formed by light. So it is light that you must love, first and foremost, and the gold will follow; it will come to you. When you walk out with the princess, all her attendants will follow you, ready to serve you. Whereas, if your head is full of gold, it will dazzle and blind you to everything else. Once the idea of money fills your head, you will have eyes for nothing else, not even for the beauty, splendour and intelligence of creation.

You will object, 'What are you talking about? We have to have money.' Believe me, I know better than you how necessary money is. But I still say that you must not fill your head with it; you must not make it your master, your ideal; you must not think that that is what life is all about. Money is a means, a tool, an agent, yes; but not an ideal, not a goal. Your ideal must be something quite different: your ideal must be light; your goal must be light. Never let money become your master; it is a very good servant but a very bad master; as your master it will give you disastrous advice and lead you away from the Kingdom of God. Keep your mind fixed on light, therefore, because, if you possess the light you will be capable of healing yourself, of achieving the mastery of yourself, of understanding the whole of life... and even gold will come your way. But if you don't possess the light, there will always be others more intelligent than you who will rob you of what you have. What else can you expect if you're so stupid?

The trouble is that people *are* stupid: they have found their attitudes at a commonplace stall in a commonplace market and now they spend their time clamouring for cash, cash and still more cash because, they say, 'If I had lots of cash I could get everything else I wanted!' Yes, everybody knows that particular stall but almost nobody knows what I know. For I also have a stall in the market and you would do better to come to my stall. You will soon see what you can buy there.

There was once a king who enjoyed strolling through the market (Nowadays, kings are so restricted, they can no longer wander through the markets by themselves but, in the old days, that was possible. A king could walk about in the town and his subjects would come and present their petitions to him). So, this king was strolling through the market and looking at the stalls when, all of a sudden, he heard a merchant shouting, 'Wisdom for sale; come and buy some wisdom!' Greatly intrigued, the king went up to the man and asked him, 'Do you really have wisdom for sale? How much is it?' 'It comes in three sizes', said the merchant, 'One hundred crowns, a thousand crowns or ten thousand crowns.' 'I'll take ten thousand crowns-worth!' said the king. 'Very well! Here you are: "Do what you have to do, but think of the consequences."' 'Is that all?' 'Yes, that's all.' The king laughed, paid the merchant his ten thousand crowns and walked off, chuckling and murmuring, 'Do what you have to do, but think of the consequences'.

By the time he got back to the palace he had forgotten the incident until, suddenly, the phrase came back into his mind: 'Do what you have to do, but think of the consequences', and he laughed again, thinking of that strange philosopher. The next morning, the king was being shaved before going to an important meeting with his ministers. His chin was already covered with shaving cream and his barber was approaching him with the razor in his hand, when he suddenly thought of the wisdom he had bought in the market and, looking at his barber, he said, jokingly, 'Do what you have to do, but think of the consequences.' To his astonishment, his barber went as white as chalk and fell at his feet, sobbing, 'Mercy, Lord; have mercy on me! I didn't want to do it; it was the ministers who forced me.' The king quickly recovered from his amazement and, realizing that some dreadful plot had been hatched against him, pretended to know about it. 'I know all that', he said, 'But tell me exactly...' 'Sire, I was meant to slit your throat while I was shaving you. I have a wife and children, sire, and they threatened me. I had to do it.' 'Yes, but who?' 'I'll tell you, sire; but promise me you won't kill me.' Well, you can imagine the rest of the story for yourselves, but this is how the king was saved, thanks to the wisdom he had bought in the market.

And I, too, have a stall in the market, but my wisdom is free. And this is what I am telling you today: 'Cherish light above everything else; cling to light and you will be saved.'

And now, just a word or two more to complete what we were saying about the servant. What does a servant — or the housewife, if she hasn't got a servant — have to do every day? She has to sweep, dust, wash and tidy her house and adorn it with some flowers here and there. But human beings have never understood the meaning of what they do every day. For me, this is a language. It is the book of Nature that I love to read and interpret. Since we are all obliged to look after the cleanliness, order and harmony of our houses, shouldn't we show the same patient care, regularity and tenacity in keeping our inner life clean and tidy?

It is this understanding that is so lacking in ordinary human beings: they focus only on the physical dimension and fail to see that cleanliness and order must also exist in their mental life; that it is on this level that they must get into the habit of making everything tidy and harmonious every day, without fail. It is this that is beautiful and useful: unfailingly, every day, to look into oneself, saying 'Let's see: what needs to be tidied up?' And then, to clean and tidy up anything that is out of place, untidy or bizarre and to get rid of any rubbish or dust that has gathered. If the disorder is not tidied up every day, it will end by becoming unmanageable. Every day, therefore, several times a day, you must try to restore peace, order and harmony within yourself. Those who fail to do so will never be in command of the situation. People hasten to repair the destruction caused by a storm, an air raid or an earthquake as soon as it is over. Why don't you do the same, every day, in your inner life? There are always some little storms going on, some rain or some bombs falling, a few holes through which mice can get in ...so there is always a little patching and cleaning and tidying to be done. You must look into yourself every day, and if you see that your thoughts and sentiments are not what they should be, you must set things straight immediately.

But people do none of this. They do nothing because they have never been taught the truths of Initiatic Science or, if they have learned these truths, they scoff at their precepts. And yet, by practising these methods a human being can achieve complete control of all his cells. Yes, because he will have understood, he will have been faithful and constant and, one day, everything will fall into place and work exactly as he wants it to. When the bombs were falling we saw how the soldiers and firemen put out the fires and repaired the bridges and so on, without delay, and we think that that is normal; we take it for granted. But when it is our own inner life that is concerned, we don't know what to do. So, now you see why we try to concentrate three, four, five, ten times a day, so as to remedy the situation. If you hear a voice setting up a great hubbub within you, tell it to keep quiet and go and sit down and listen. And persevere until you succeed in making it obey you. You will be proud of yourself when you gain the upper hand. But if you let everything go and expect the situation to sort itself out alone, peace and tranquillity will not be restored for years... if ever.

There; now you see what interesting conclusions we can draw from this image of the lady of the house and her maid.

Sèvres, March 22, 1962

II

The Master reads the Meditation for the day:

'The poor don't know how to use their poverty as the most effective means of evolution; they constantly rebel against it. Why? Because they want the money that the rich have. They would like others to think that they find wealth offensive but, in fact, they long for it with all their might. If the rich had a clearer understanding of the question, they would distribute all their wealth to the poor, and the poor would refuse it and say, "No, no; we don't want anything; we're very well off just as we are!" If they were truly enlightened, the rich would want to strip themselves of their wealth and the poor would want nothing more than they have. For the sake of their own salvation, therefore, the rich should turn to the poor and beg them to accept their riches, and the poor should refuse adamantly. You will say that I'm turning everything upside down. Exactly! Because this is how we can get everything right side up again!'

How people would scoff at the idea that the rich should offer their wealth to the poor and the poor should refuse it! So why do I talk about it? Is it for your amusement and my own? No. Be patient and you will hear some very interesting explanations.

Can the rich or the poor explain the reason for their circumstances? Do they know why some people are rich and others poor? If you ask a priest he will tell you that it is the will of God. What have the rich done to deserve their fortune and the poor to deserve their poverty? Nobody can answer this because they have rejected the notion of reincarnation which explains every individual situation. Those who are rich today have earned their wealth, in one way or another, in previous incarnations. Initiatic Science tells us that, sooner or later, we always get what we ask for. Whether what you ask for be good or bad, you will get it. The Lord gives every creature what they ask Him for, and if it turns out to be bad for them, it is not His fault. If you ask for a burden and then find yourself crushed beneath its weight, you cannot blame the Lord. It is a terrible thing not to foresee the long-term consequences of what you ask for. If you knew in advance how things would turn out, if you foresaw that the satisfaction of your desires would lead to unhappiness or illness, you wouldn't ask for them. This is why, in Initiatic Science, the disciples begin by learning that some things should be asked for and others should not.

In any case, one thing is certain, and that is that the rich are rich because they have cultivated certain qualities and worked for their wealth. The law is always faithful and true. You will say, 'But they cheated and lied. They got rich by fraud and violence'. That may well be, but, even if they did use such means, the law says that they must be given wealth because they have done everything in their power to get it. Of course, what the law does not say is whether they will keep their wealth for long nor whether it will satisfy them and give them peace and joy. But they will get what they asked for. They may have succeeded by using illicit means, but they have succeeded. What they don't know, of course, is what the consequences of their success will be. To be sure, not all the rich have used deceit and dishonesty to achieve wealth. Some have become rich through their own hard work or thanks to an inheritance, by chance or thanks to a discovery. It is not possible to enumerate each particular case.

Take the case of the Jews, for instance: most of the major businesses are in their hands today. And who made this situation possible? Christians. In their ignorance and hatred, Christians persecuted the Jews and this persecution led to their developing some exceptional qualities that enabled them to survive even in the worst conditions. It is true that a practice such as circumcision (which is based on an age-old science), through the modifications it produces in the functioning of the endocrine glands, has contributed to a particular trend in the evolution of Jews. But it is Christians who, without realizing it, drove the Jews to develop their financial skills and, today, it is they who rule the world. To be sure, there are also Christians and Muslims who have become immensely rich through the oil industry but none of them has the abilities and that special intelligence that Jews have. In one way or another, therefore, the rich have earned their wealth.

And now, let's talk about Initiates. Initiates have no desire to be rich because their aim is not to settle down in the world nor to rule over it. An Initiate wants, above all, to become a luminous beacon, a shining light and, consequently, he has no wish to encumber himself with things that would prevent him from devoting himself to this divine task. An Initiate wants to be free and detached in order to work on himself and others; it is because he refuses to burden himself that he is able to make continual progress and go from strength to strength until he becomes truly formidable. He doesn't need to worry about protecting his money from thieves, falling prices on the stock exchange or the devaluation of the franc or the dollar. This is why I say that those who are always in hot pursuit of wealth are fools: they don't understand that, because of this, their soul will never know anything but emptiness. What good will it do them to swallow up the whole world? It would be different if they used some of their wealth to help very gifted young people to become outstanding artists or scientists, for instance. But, no; they keep it all for themselves and never help anyone; they are only interested in opening more and more branch offices or shops and ruining their competitors. And, as they know nothing of the laws, they don't know that, when they come back to earth in their next reincarnation, they will be beggars.

Believe me, many of the beggars we see everywhere today are the reincarnation of people who were very rich in a previous incarnation but who were also very selfish and tight-fisted. It is good to be rich. Yes, but it is only good to be rich if it allows you to be useful to others, not if it means that you despoil them and give a free rein to your craving for destruction. So many people use the power their money gives them to pull strings behind the scenes and do all kinds of despicable things. If they only knew what they were storing up for themselves! But they don't care one jot about that: they have other irons in the fire. And this is why, one day, the Invisible World will decide to pull the floor out from under their feet and let them all collapse. And they will collapse – all of them. The time is drawing near. The Invisible World gives each human being the chance to manifest himself, and all that he does is recorded until, having given a free rein to his basest inclinations for long enough, the time comes for him to be judged. And the laws are terrible! This is what human beings don't realize. They live in darkness and, even when great Masters come to enlighten them, they reject them and refuse to believe what they say.

Of course, anyone can see that: all those great Masters, all those Initiates who have dedicated their lives to discovering truth, who have made such great sacrifices and proved their absolute disinterestedness, kindness and greatness of soul – they are all misguided. It is the idiots, brutes and criminals of this world that are on the right track. No, no; believe me, nothing could be further from the truth! In fact, I will show you that you don't know how to read the book of living nature; you have never learned to read the language of plants, mountains, lakes and animals – or of mankind. Let me give you just one example out of thousands: when the sun rises who sees it first? Those who are at the bottom of a canyon or those who are on top of a mountain? Those at the top of the mountain, of course. In other words, it is those who are purest, most noble and most elevated who are the first to see and grasp the great truths. Goodness knows how many hundreds of years it will be before the common run of benighted fools begins to grasp a few smatterings as well. This image of the mountain tops lit by the first rays of the rising sun is a lesson. The great book of Nature is laid out before us and we have to decipher and interpret it; we shall never be misled if we do this. Most human beings trample this book underfoot, that is why they are so deeply plunged into error and illusion.

Go and look at all those who set out to swallow up the whole world and see what a state they are in a few years later: they are preparing to end their days in clinics or asylums because their nervous system cannot stand the strain. They believed that wealth would give them security, pleasure and power, and it does give them these things; that's true. Unfortunately, it also gives them something else. They are constantly harassed and have nothing solid to hold on to inwardly. But Initiates, whose only desire is for light, love and purity, live in a state of total fulfilment. Their only concern — apart from the barest necessities in the way of food, clothing and shelter — is how to help others. No one is happier than they and yet, instead of imitating them, the poor spend their time moaning and envying the rich. They fail to understand that their poverty gives them spiritual conditions that could help them to discover another world and to dedicate themselves to a sublime ideal. They are free but, as they don't know how to use their freedom, they are no better than the rich and are just as much to be pitied.

I know, of course, that the rich will never beg the poor to relieve them of their riches. Nor will the poor refuse the invitation. The idea is ludicrous. But I simply wanted to make the point that a rich man is so weighed down by his burden of wealth that he needs to be relieved of some of that weight. Look at how he walks: shoulders bowed and hands behind his back, his fingers constantly moving as though they were automatically counting. And, as he never looks where he's going, he stumbles against a branch and falls down. And a poor man who is an idealist is no better off: walking along with his head in the clouds and not looking where he is going, he ends by tumbling into a ditch. You have to be sensible and learn to look both up and down while you're walking. A whole philosophy is contained in the way one walks.

Actually, if the rich really wanted to live a sensible and more balanced life, they would make up their minds to get rid of part of their burden. Yes, but as the poor would be perfectly content as they are, they would not want to saddle themselves with any extra weight. And I find myself in the same situation: even if a multi-millionaire offered me several millions, I would tell him, 'No, I don't need it. Give it to the Brotherhood if you like but, personally, I prefer to be free and to go on with my work.' I feel myself to be the richest of men; why should I impoverish myself? But people just don't understand: true wealth lies in being at peace and seeing things as they really are. What value is there in the possession of wealth if it is to the detriment of all that is most precious in yourself? True wealth is the wealth of your thoughts and feelings, for you can share them with others without impoverishing yourself.

It is good to possess material wealth but only on condition that it does not rob you of your freedom. I have already explained this question in a previous lecture. When the Pharisees and Sadducees were looking for a pretext to condemn Jesus, they asked him, 'Is it lawful to pay taxes to Caesar, or not?' But Jesus asked for a coin and said, 'Whose image and inscription is this?' 'Caesar's.' And Jesus said, 'Render therefore to Caesar the things that are Caesar's, and to God the things that are God's.'

For two thousand years Christians have been quoting this saying and yet they have never discovered how much they should render to Caesar and how much to God. And then I come on the scene with my warped mentality and, setting fire to a log of wood I say, 'Look how it burns: first it produces masses of

flames; then it produces gasses, in lesser quantities; then a little
water vapour, even less; and, finally, all that disappears and we
are left with nothing but a handful of ashes. Well, the ashes are
for Caesar because they are all that is left on the ground.' That
is what Caesar is: the ground. Caesar is here, on earth. The flames,
gasses and steam that go up into the sky belong to Heaven. So,
there you are: we must consecrate three quarters of all our possessions, activities, thoughts and sentiments to the Lord and one
quarter to Caesar; nothing could be more clear. But, instead of
that, people give all they have got to Caesar and keep nothing
for the Lord. This is why the rich will be punished, if not in their
present incarnation, then in the next. And if you say, 'I don't
give a hoot about being punished in my next incarnation; I mean
to have as much as I can in this one!' all I can say is that you
are very stupid to take that attitude.

For my part, I have always maintained that, if I were offered
the earth itself on condition that I gave up my work, I would
refuse. Yes, because, if I were deprived of these spiritual activities,
I would be dead; I would have no taste for life any more. So,
my answer is, 'Keep all your money and leave me alone'. Believe
me, I say this before Heaven, and Heaven knows that it is the
truth. So many people allow themselves to be bought without
hesitation. This is why the rich are convinced of only one thing:
that everything can be bought. And, in fact, it is all too true:
they buy men's convictions, feelings and consciences. If you only
knew what went on in the world, you would realize how powerful money was. Money is all-powerful on earth. Yes, but it has
no value at all in the world above. There are other things that
are all-powerful in the world above, not money. And this is why,
if your ideal is to become exceptional beings, you must be more
and more ready to refuse certain commitments, certain responsibilities, knowing that, if you don't refuse them, it will mean losing
your liberty.

True wisdom lies in being capable of giving up certain things.
But it is as though people's one desire was to allow themselves

to be enslaved on every level. Not long ago a woman came and asked for my advice about remarrying: she had already divorced six husbands and was contemplating getting married for the seventh time. I was dumbfounded! I said to her, 'Dear lady, don't you attach any importance to your freedom?' No; it seems that freedom bored her; she felt that she should always be married, always unhappy and ready to divorce again. Why couldn't she take advantage of her freedom to undertake some new spiritual activities? People always seem to feel the need to tie themselves down. In fact, nine tenths of you are in the same situation: you have the mentality of the rich. Instead of freeing yourselves so as to devote yourselves to making fantastic discoveries, you go in search of situations or occupations that will effectively bury you and prevent you from learning anything about true wealth.

Half of my life has been spent in poverty and privations of all kinds and it is thanks to these conditions that I have been able to practise and make so many experiments. Everybody thinks that, if only they had a little laboratory somewhere, they could do all kinds of experiments. They don't realize that they have the best and most perfectly equipped laboratory in themselves: their whole being. And they take this laboratory with them wherever they go. When I understood that I possessed this laboratory, I started to do thousands of experiments – and I still do so. Whereas, if I had been rich, I might well have led a life of ostentatious pleasure and profligacy. Why not? That is what wealth leads to. At least, if you are not rich, you are not in the same danger. Wealth is a great temptation; you have to be very strong to live in opulence and have a spiritual life as intense as it would be if you were poor. Why do you think hermits went to live in the desert? Why are monks required to take the vow of poverty? Because an authentic spiritual life requires a great deal of self-renunciation and inner effort and wealth is not the condition most conducive to this.

I make no secret of my ambition to become the richest man on earth – spiritually speaking, that is. You will say that this

is excessive. Not at all; I am only exercising the right that the
Lord has given to each one of us, to become richer, more intelligent and more powerful than anyone else. He tells us, even
commands us, to do so, for Jesus said, 'Therefore you shall be
perfect, just as your Father in heaven is perfect.' The Lord is the
richest, the wisest and the most beautiful of all; He is the noblest
and the purest, and we have not only the right but the duty to
resemble Him. So, there you are: my ambition is to become
perfect. This is my God-given right. It is only narrow-minded,
ignorant human beings who wax indignant and declare that it is
insufferable pride on my part. No, to want to be perfect is not
pride; it is something quite different.

As you see, as the days go by, more and more notions get
straightened out in your minds.

The Bonfin, July 18, 1978

*

*   *

My dear brothers and sisters, so many errors are possible
without this Initiatic knowledge. Nowhere else will you hear that
the reason for poverty and wealth can often be traced back to
previous incarnations and that many of today's beggars and down-
and-outs are people who once used their wealth for evil purposes.
Faced with this problem of inequality in men's fortunes, a Christian will say, 'It's God's will'. Yes, that is how they envisage the
will of God: as an injustice, a purely arbitrary decision.

One day, Mullah Nashrudin[1] came into the village pub with a sackful of walnuts. He had several walnut trees in his garden and was in a generous mood — a rare occurrence in his life — so he had decided to share his nuts with his friends. Some of them were probably inedible already, but no matter! Anyway, he comes in at the door, dumps his sack on the floor and shouts, 'Ho, there, my friends, I have some nuts for you. How shall I distribute them, as the Lord distributes His gifts or as men distribute theirs?' Naturally, everybody was convinced that the Lord showed greater justice than men, so they told him to do as the Lord does. 'Right!' says Mullah Nashrudin and, picking up his sack, he goes to the first man and gives him one nut. Then, passing in front of several others without giving them anything, he stops and empties the entire contents in front of the last man. 'Hey, Nashrudin', they all shout, 'That's not fair! It's unjust!' 'But that is exactly how the Lord distributes things' says Mullah Nashrudin, 'He gives nothing to some and everything to others!' And this is how the Church understands the question.

The truth is that God has given everything to all of us: water, air, warmth, light and even the prâna and all kinds of beneficial elements that exist on the subtle planes. And, that being so, why are we still so poor and indigent? Because we don't know how to capture and absorb those elements. Only Initiates know how to do this. Everyone else thinks that life is poor, that the Lord has not given them anything. But He has, He has given them everything; everything is theirs for the taking. It is just that they are too spineless and lazy, too stupid and too blind to see it, so they remain poor. It is human beings themselves that restrict themselves so severely. They are content to eat, drink and breathe, that is to say to feed on the solid, liquid and gaseous elements, but they ignore the fiery elements, fire and light. This is why mankind is degenerating: because it is not properly nourished. To be properly nourished we need all four elements and this means

1 Mullah Nashrudin, the name of a popular figure of fun in Turkish folklore.

that it is very important to be present as the sun rises, so as to
see and absorb the fire and light that pours from it in such abundance every day. Fire is the most essential of the four elements.

It is possible to go without food for several days: prisoners
who went on a hunger-strike have held out for as long as sixty
days. To go without drinking is more difficult; you cannot do
without water for more than a few days. To go without air is
even more difficult; you can't stop breathing for more than three
or four minutes at most. And fire? 'That's easy', you might say,
'I've survived a whole winter without a fire!' Yes, you can get
along without heating in winter, perhaps, but I'm not talking
about external warmth; I'm talking about the warmth of the heart.
The instant a man's heart loses its warmth, he dies. Of all the
four elements, the one that is most important for life is fire. But
human beings are bent on dissipating this sacred fire, this warmth,
in their pleasures and follies and, in this way, they are shorten-
ing their lives. If they knew how to preserve this fire, they would
live for centuries.

A human being can be compared to a multi-stage rocket. When
all the fuel in the first stage has been used, the burners in the
second stage are lit and, when the second lot of fuel is exhausted,
the third stage fires and so on; in this way, the rocket can continue in flight for a long time. When a man dies, therefore, it
means that he has failed to fire the burners in the next stage. He
could have lived longer, for he still has some fuel left.

Everything is at our disposal: God has filled the atmosphere
and the rivers, lakes and mountains of the world, even the stars,
with everything we need. He has kept nothing back for Himself.
But, as human beings are incapable of reaching out to grasp all
this wealth, they remain poor and miserable. Try, henceforth,
through meditation and contemplation, to reach up to the highest
planes so as to garner some of these elements. They are there,
waiting for you; there are no 'Keep out' signs up there. The 'Keep
out' signs are in you, because you are not strong, pure and intelligent enough. Believe me, everything you need is there, ready

and waiting for you if you are capable of reaching out for it. Light, warmth, space, the stars — they are all at our disposal. It is we who fail to use them. The Lord distributes everything; no one is more generous than Him.

Take life, for example: life is present all around us in water, in rocks and trees and, above all, in the air and the sun, but we die because our bodies are unable to draw on that life. God is just and supremely generous; He has never said that His riches were for some and not for others. If we have never done anything to enable us to benefit from them, it is not His fault. This is why we have to study and train ourselves, otherwise we shall go through one incarnation after another in the same condition of poverty and misery and the same attitude of recrimination against the Lord. The thing that really amazes me is that Christians can continue to believe in a God as monstrous as they conceive Him to be. They pray to Him and love Him but, in their ignorance, they have invented a monster. No other Teaching glorifies God as much as ours does. Look around you and you will see the strange notions other Teachings try to give you.

The Bonfin, August 15, 1978

Chapter Seven

Aristocracy and Democracy

I

The Master reads the Meditation for the day:

'A human being is inhabited by a whole population of cells which are directly dependent on him and, consequently, strongly influenced by him. This is why they imitate him in everything. If a person habitually transgresses the law, his population notices this and becomes exactly like its master, and it is on his head that any repercussions fall. He feels that something is not quite right and complains: 'What's wrong with me? There's a revolution going on inside me!' The truth is that it is he who has taught his cells to behave in this way.

All your ailments are the result of the bad upbringing you have given your cells. You do nothing but grumble as you sweep your room; you knock the chairs about, kick your doors shut, bump into the furniture − and your cells imitate you. When they have to move something they kick it, and you cry out in pain and wonder what is going on. Well, it is simply some of your cells kicking the furniture about in imitation of your own behaviour.'

What and where is that furniture? What a strange text that is; all about our cells kicking things about!

Of course, those who don't know what a human being is or

how he is constructed and who don't know that he is inhabited
by millions of microscopic creatures will find the whole idea absurd. They don't realize that our cells are tiny intelligent souls;
they are a population, a people with whom we are in constant
contact. They are our children, our pupils, and we have to teach
and guide them. But the trouble is that we don't know them and
never bother about them, with the result that they don't obey us.
However much we plead or threaten, they refuse to budge. Take
the question of sexuality, for instance: a man can be a pastor,
a bishop or anything else you like to imagine, but his sexual organs
function as they please, they don't listen to him. An Initiate, on
the other hand, who is aware of certain truths and certain rules,
knows how to command the cells of his organs so that they obey
him. Yes, because he is fully conscious and has learned to communicate with them.

In the passage I read a moment ago, I used the example of
people who slam doors and kick the furniture. If human beings
were more sensitive and if they analysed themselves, they would
notice that all this banging about, all the noise and commotion
they cause outwardly, is reflected in their inner being. Admit-
tedly, your tables and chairs have neither souls nor consciousness,
but human beings have; they have souls and a psychic life and
all this tumult, all those chaotic gestures are reflected in their
psychic life. If they were sensitive they would feel the effects of
this confusion, disruption and disharmony, for our gestures
reverberate not only in our brain but in our whole being. The
significance of our gestures, in fact, constitutes a science in itself.
Every gesture is an eloquent expression not only of a person's
inner attitude, decisions and intentions but also of his level of
evolution.

A human being is home to a whole population, therefore,
but, as he doesn't know it, he never does anything to care for
them or improve their lot. He is more concerned with the world
around him and never gives a thought to the world he carries
within him and of which he is the educator and master. And

yet the events that go on inside a human being are a replica of what goes on in society. We see the same unrest and up-heavals, the same revolutions. Human history tells of many kings who proved to be unfit to rule and were overthrown by their subjects. Knowing nothing about the terrible laws of karma, they reigned over their people with cruelty and injustice and, all the while, secretly and silently, others plotted their downfall and, eventually, toppled them from their thrones. There are any number of examples of this: kings who were dethroned and thrown into dungeons where they lived miserably for years on a diet of bread and water, constantly hoping to be freed, while those who had seized power ruled in their stead. Every-body has heard of such happenings but how many understand that the same things go on in their own inner life? The king within us slips into slothful or licentious habits, leaving the way open to hostile forces which seize him, throw him into prison and start to rule in his place.

Human beings must regain their place at the head of their kingdom, therefore, otherwise they will end by being completely supplanted by thieves and bandits from amongst their own citizens. If a person is unjust and dishonest, if he fails to respect certain laws, the inevitable result is an inner revolution that top-ples him from power and puts the reins of government into the hands of monsters. And his friends and neighbours are so blind that they don't even notice that it is not the same person who is in command. Of course, there are extreme cases in which no one can help seeing it: if someone begins to say, 'I'm Genghis Khan, or Jesus Christ, or Napoleon Bonaparte', it becomes obvi-ous that he has been replaced. It is certainly neither Genghis Khan nor Napoleon nor, above all, Jesus Christ who has usurped his place! But he himself, poor fellow, has no idea where he is. The phenomenon of the dual personality is widely recognized today; no one doubts that it exists. But what people don't know is that this dual – or rather this multiple – personality exists in every one of us. Yes, because man is inhabited by millions of different spirits and entities which can all manifest themselves in their different ways depending on circumstances.

Believe me, there are rules in the inner world just as there are in the outer world, and it is important to know them. Why do people think that they can use injustice, violence and cruelty in order to dominate others indefinitely without their retaliating? Even terror will not keep people down or force them to submit to atrocities for ever. All those who thought otherwise have learned a terrible lesson. In fact, this is why the aristocracy was brought down and replaced by democracy. Not that this means that democracy is better. It would have been far better if the aristocracy had been capable of remaining in charge by reason of its qualities of intelligence and nobility of character for, symbolically speaking, the aristocracy is the brain, that which is at the top, which sees and foresees and rules, whereas democracy is the common people, the stomach, belly and sexual organs.

I have often given you the example of a ship with its captain on the bridge and its stokers in the engine rooms. The stokers are the common people and they have the ability to drive the ship, but they cannot see where they are going; if they were allowed to steer, their mistakes could be disastrous. But, although it would be a grave mistake to underestimate their importance – they represent the means, the conditions, the energy that is so necessary – they cannot be entrusted with functions that belong only to the captain, to the aristocracy. The masses are incapable of making intelligent decisions and steering events in the right direction. Forgive me for saying so, but that is the truth. The cells of the stomach have not been given the capacity to instruct and guide the others. When the stomach or the sexual organs clamour for something, the brain must not hasten to give in to them and satisfy their demands without a second thought. Human beings must be guided and enlightened by wisdom, and the strength and energy of the masses is there to realize the splendours that are the fruits of wisdom.

You will say, 'But all that is very dangerous! It's dangerous

to condemn democracy and speak in favour of the aristocracy.'
Well, there is danger in everything we do. When you eat and drink
you are in danger of being poisoned or of choking to death. When
you go out into the street you are in danger of being hit on the
head by a tile falling from a roof. We are surrounded by dangers
of every kind, but we have to speak the truth. And the truth is
that it would be better to restore an enlightened aristocracy than
to be ruled by the judgment and appetites of an ignorant populace.
Naturally, I am well aware that there are some genuine aristocrats
amongst the masses, people with the highest ideals and aspirations. I have met any number of them: they have neither titles
nor mansions nor insignia of any kind, but the extraordinary
generosity and selflessness of their lives set them apart as the best
type of aristocrat. I believe that you are beginning to understand
me now, aren't you?

When the world begins to listen to this aristocracy of élite beings, it will mean the transformation of everything. It will be the
masses themselves that will clamour for a government of the
aristocracy, for they will recognize that, left to their own resources,
without the light they need, they can only lose their way.

But a hierarchical order must exist within each human being:
every human being should have the aristocracy here, in his head,
and the masses here, in his stomach. Both are necessary, but if
you get them mixed up and allow them to exchange places, sooner
or later it will lead to disaster. The solution is for every human
being to implore Heaven to send an aristocracy of luminous beings into his head to guide and instruct him. This won't prevent
the democracy from carrying out its duties; on the contrary, it
must go on working even at night, for if the masses stop working, if the work of digestion, circulation and elimination ceases,
the whole body, including the aristocracy, will be doomed.

What harm is there, therefore, in telling you that you must
get back your throne and be a king again; that you must achieve
self-mastery and learn to renounce certain weaknesses in order
to escape the clutches of the wild beasts within you? There is no

more important work than this: to become king of your own inner realm and gain the love, respect and obedience of your citizens. If they see that you are a good ruler, they will make an effort to do whatever you ask. If some of them start to lose their temper, you only have to say, 'No, no; calm down!' and they will obey you. Otherwise, if you are not in command, you will have to wait for days; they will calm down when they feel like it and there will be nothing you can do about it. The same is true for your sexual energy: if you have learned self-discipline, your cells will become disciplined, too. But if you have learned nothing, you will be obliged to satisfy their demands, otherwise they will overpower you. This is what happens when you are not in command: you are ruled by others that you know nothing about.

You have never envisaged the question in these terms before, have you? You live like everybody else: unconsciously. But that won't do! From now on, you must be conscious of what goes on inside you, because you have a duty towards your inhabitants. They have been entrusted to your care so that you can employ them in a work of great importance, and all you do is set them a bad example! When you have to meet other people socially you take care to be impeccable: your words, gestures, expressions and clothes are all perfect. But when you are alone and no one can see you it is quite another matter; you let yourself go and never think about the inner population that is watching you. Seeing this, they say to themselves, 'Very well, if that's the example he gives us, we'll do the same. He'll soon see what it's like!' and, before you know what has happened, power has been wrested from you. Whereas if you behave well in front of your citizens, they are capable of doing wonders for you.

If you realized what an immense population dwelt in you, you would take great pride in it. There are billions and billions of them – more than the total population of the world. And let me tell you that some Initiates have been so successful in educating the entities that dwell in them and have helped them to become so strong and so highly evolved, that they are now capable of working by themselves: they go and help, console and heal their master's friends and disciples. Sometimes, indeed, when they go to help others, they take on the appearance of the Initiate, and this is why people think that it was he who visited them whereas, in fact, he is often the last to learn that he has helped someone.

Yes, if a human being works intelligently and consciously, he can strengthen some of his inner entities to such a degree and give them such powers that, although he himself cannot go absolutely everywhere, thanks to these entities, he can travel throughout the world to enlighten all creatures and prepare the coming of the Kingdom of God. Believe me, this is the absolute truth, but it is a truth that orthodox science has never even suspected – still less accepted. Even the Russians, who have done a lot of work on parapsychological phenomena such as clairvoyance, the aura and the etheric body, still do not know this. The truth is that man's possibilities are unimaginable, indescribable and virtually unlimited, but they depend, of course, on his degree of evolution. If someone decides to study, to achieve self-mastery and to overcome certain failings, all those possibilities are there before him, ready and waiting. I am not the first to tell you this. What I am saying has been said before by all Initiates and all Masters since the world began. I am not inventing anything. I am here simply to transmit the secret of their learning and their power and to lead you, little by little, towards all that splendour.

If a disciple makes up his mind to work in this direction, therefore, Heaven takes him under Its wing and his own inhabitants give him more and more help and support. There are even doctors and healers amongst them who take care of his health. The fact that certain people can reach a very great age without falling ill shows that some of their inner entities look after their health, for health does not depend only on our organs; it depends on the entities that live in them and animate them. And, if these entities are weak or become paralysed, it only remains for us to put ourselves in the hands of the pharmacists, doctors and surgeons. And there is no telling whether or not they will be capable of healing us or prolonging our life!

This is exactly what goes on at night when, without our being aware of it, thousands of entities work to help our organism to rid itself of its toxins and replenish its forces. If these entities are absent or if they are hindered in their work, you will not be refreshed, even after a night's sleep. If you always rely on external means instead of turning to these intelligent entities, if you never ask them to help you or show them the appreciation they need to do their work properly, you can spend your life in pursuit of healing but, as you don't understand what it really means nor who it is that heals, you will never achieve it. Let me give you an example: you have a machine of some kind that has broken down and, as it can't mend itself, you call a mechanic to come and mend it. But human beings, who constantly experience problems of this nature in their daily lives, have never understood that the situation is exactly the same in themselves.

Believe me, as long as you continue to reject this philosophy, you will never find the solution to your problems, whether they be medical, economic or educational. You must respect and appreciate all these intelligent workers who live within you, for when they see that you treat them with love and gratitude, they will do their work magnificently and you will always feel healthy and even-tempered; nothing will be lacking.

Yes, the external world in which we live contains all kinds of lessons that we must learn to decipher. The example of the machine that breaks down is so clear: it takes a mechanic to get it working again. In the same way, our organs have to be repaired and kept in working order by living entities. A man's organs can be in good shape but, if those who animate them have been ordered to leave, he dies. The machine stops working, even though its organs are intact — and this can be seen in the fact that the organs of his dead body can be grafted onto someone else's body. It is simply that those who kept the machine running have left, so it has stopped. But suppose it had been decreed that a man was to live for two or three hundred years, his organs would continue to function because they would constantly be fuelled and kept alive by new particles and new entities.

Actually, the human physical body is capable of living for thousands of years. Of course, this is only possible in exceptional circumstances and by a special decree of Providence; generally speaking, owing to the inevitable flaws in their heredity, human beings cannot live much more than a hundred years. But, even if you don't want to live for several hundred years, it is always possible to work to be stronger and healthier. And the only way to do this is to rely on what is alive and not on what is dead, because only living elements have the power to heal. What happens, for instance, if you have an abscess or an open sore? Where are the entities that know how to heal the sore or clean all the impurities from the abscess? If they have been chloroformed and driven away by your chaotic way of life, the infection in your sore or abscess will get worse and turn into tetanus or gangrene and then you will have to have your leg cut off. All because you have banished the specialized workers who could have healed you. Even though you do everything possible externally, with disinfectants, salves and dressings, the sore will still get infected.

You must understand that the most effective remedies come from within and that, if your inner entities are not allowed to do their work properly, external remedies are powerless to compensate. Conversely, if your inner entities are in good shape, your organism will heal itself, even if there is no outside help available. So, you see, it is all very simple, very clear: you must change your mentality and give first place to the psychic, spiritual dimension; and, above all, you must work to achieve complete control and mastery of yourself so as to reign over your inner population and do good to all around you. Is this possible? Yes, it is. And you will take pride in having fulfilled the mission with which you were sent down to earth: to become a model of integrity, honesty and purity.

You now understand, I am sure, that when I talk about the

aristocracy, I am referring to that inner aristocracy that we all possess but which has been toppled from power because it was not equal to its task. This aristocracy has continued to rule in a few, very exceptional cases, in the great philosophers, sages and Initiates. In them, because it is the head that rules, their populace, the cells of the stomach, belly and sexual organs, etc., obey them and work magnificently.

To be sure, all this is beyond the reach of most human beings. They are filled with every imaginable purpose except that of becoming exemplary human beings, true servants of God, conductors of light. And yet, how easy it would be to give them the means to achieve this! The difficulty lies in getting them to aspire to such an ideal. Even the Lord is incapable of giving men this desire; they have to acquire it for themselves. Just as no one can eat in another person's place, no one can aspire to something in their place, either. I give you food, but it is you who have to eat it. If I ate it for you, I would get fatter and you would get thinner. But disciples are an extraordinary breed: they think that their Master should do everything and they themselves nothing. They even want their Master to provide them with love, will-power and perseverance. Unfortunately, for them, nothing of the kind exists in Initiatic Science.

A Master gives his disciples the means, the methods and the conditions he needs, but it is up to him to do the work, otherwise he will end up in the same situation as the lazy man in the story. It happened, one day, in Turkey: a peasant was digging a ditch and, as it was very hard work, each time he thrust his spade into the ground, he grunted, 'Oof! oof!' A lazy good-for-nothing happened to pass by and, seeing the man digging, he said, 'Why don't we share the work? You do the digging and I'll do the 'Oof-ing', and then we'll share the wages, too.' 'Agreed!' said the peasant. So there they were, one digging and the other going 'Oof! Oof!'. Of course, when the peasant received his money and kept it all for himself, the other man was furious and brought him up before the *cadi* (the village magistrate). When the magistrate had heard the story, he said, 'You're right; it's only fair to share.' Turning to the peasant, he said, 'Bring me the coins that you received as wages.' When these were handed to him, the magistrate took them and dropped them on the floor, one by one, then, giving them back to the peasant, he said to the lazy man, 'Since it was you who did the "Oof-ing", the clink of the coins is for you; but he did the digging, so the coins themselves are for him.' There; that is what will happen to those who expect to receive everything without working for it.

I can give you knowledge, but the good-will must come from you and the two combined will produce unheard-of results. Every day, the luminous spirits of nature will come to you to help you; every day, you will enter deeper and deeper into this extraordinary philosophy; every day, you will become freer and freer and freer.

The Bonfin, September 14, 1975

II

A great number of today's books, films, magazines and shows lead people in the direction of disorder, anarchy and chaos. And they are tremendously popular! It is astonishing to see to what extent human nature needs to feed on such diabolical stuff. So much so that you cannot really blame artists and writers for giving the public this kind of food; they are simply trying to provide what it demands so avidly. It is not entirely their fault therefore, but even so, if they had been taught by Initiates, they would know that they must not stoop to satisfy the baser appetites and lusts of men's lower nature. They would stay on a higher level and, in this way, the public would be forced to rise in order to reach them and to reach the higher intelligence and beauty that they possess. Instead of this, in trying to satisfy the masses, the *demos*, the stomach, they have helped to supplant the aristocracy of the brain, with the result that it is now men's lower nature that has the upper hand and flaunts itself, lays down the law and imposes its will.

Oh yes; we are all very 'democratic' nowadays; the masses rule; ignorance holds sway, and intelligence, the aristocracy, has been defeated because it was incapable of retaining its superiority. The time has come to form, once again, an intellectual, moral and spiritual aristocracy so that the masses may evolve. Those who are now in control — the *demos*, the stomach, the belly and the sexual organs — must allow the head to rule, for it is not for the head to gratify the desires of the belly and the sexual organs.

To be sure, if democracy has taken power, it is because the aristocracy has degenerated, just as the social and political aristocracy degenerated. To be an aristocrat does not mean to possess a name, a title, a prominent position or great estates; it means to have high personal standards of morality, generosity and strength of character.

People wanted to get rid of the monarchy and the aristocracy, to do away with tsars and nobles... Yes, but those who are now in power, even in Communist countries, perpetrate the same crimes as the overlords of old, and, once again, popular uprisings will liquidate them in their turn, because they, too, are unworthy: they have forgotten that they overthrew the monarchy and the nobility in order to establish the reign of brotherhood and justice. With the passing of the years they have forgotten their ideal and become materialized and corrupt, just as the Church, in the course of the centuries, has forgotten the principles of love taught by Jesus and become materialized.

It is time, now, to restore the aristocracy of the heart and soul, the aristocracy of the Initiates and great Masters, of all those truly enlightened beings who have proved their worth. Words are not enough. Everybody is capable of making wonderful speeches, but how many are capable of putting their words into practice? As long as those who rule and are in command are not enlightened by Initiatic Science, what good can come of their decisions? They may not actually spark bloody confrontations but nor will they produce a veritable transformation of mentalities. You only have to open your eyes and see this for yourself: do the majority of human beings demand spiritual, divine riches? No; all they ask for is money, pleasure and the freedom to indulge themselves like animals. All their demands are for their belly and stomach, never for light. In these conditions, how can you expect the masses to change the world and bring about the Kingdom of God? When they begin to ask for something more, yes, perhaps; but it is not by making some minor changes on the economic, material, financial or political level that they will bring about any great transformations. It will always be the same old story; always the same filth. The trouble is that no one has yet understood what it is that has to be changed.

True, talk of change is on everyone's lips, but all I see are the tireless endeavours of a handful of ambitious men who are bent on getting to the top so as to have more power and more money. They don't prepare themselves, they don't work to become purer and nobler or to achieve self-mastery, to become examples for others. That is not what interests them. What use would it be to them to be better human beings? That is not what they need. They need a position of power, the opportunity to gratify their passions and their thirst for conquests and revenge. This is why the world will never know peace.

The truth is that present-day society is so unenlightened that it encourages all the baser tendencies of its members. Parents are so ignorant that they think that their duty as educators is to bring up their children to look for favours and privileges in life. Instead of teaching their children to prepare themselves for their future responsibilities, so that they will be worthy of them and fulfil them with integrity, they force the most pernicious advice on them and are elated when they meet with outward success, even if it is not deserved. People's ambitions are always confined to the material plane and since, in order to succeed, one has to use cunning, deceit and violence, they end by destroying all that is best in their character.

Human beings have no difficulty in understanding that wealth makes it possible for them to influence events and reverse certain situations but, as it is rarely through honesty and generosity that they become rich — rather the contrary — they are ready to transgress every law to obtain that wealth. You will say, 'That's all very well, but if we followed your advice and spent all our time preparing and strengthening ourselves and becoming examples, conditions in the world are such that we would always be unknown and stuck away in some obscure job at the bottom of the ladder.' What makes you so sure? If you are capable and truly exceptional, if you are truly a model, a sun, whether you like it or not, others will come and fetch you, by force if necessary, and place you at their head to rule and guide them. If this has not yet happened, it is because you have not earned it; you are not yet sufficiently perfect.

Human beings are in need of true light, true science and true power. They need these things and are constantly in search of them, but, as those they frequent are not always shining examples, they get along as best they can, using dishonesty and violence in order to succeed at all costs. Inwardly, they all need something sublime but, as they never meet that something, they become discouraged and begin to imitate the brigands and vultures that surround them, telling themselves – like so many others – 'Virtue is never rewarded', 'An honest man dies of hunger' and 'Man is a wild beast for his fellow men'. In this way, each individual descends to the level of those around him and conforms to the lowest common denominator.

But if, in the future, some human beings embrace this Teaching, struggle against the general trend and sacrifice everything else for the sake of this sublime ideal, you would soon see that others would love and appreciate them and seek them out. And this is how the Kingdom of God will be established on earth. If it has not already come, it is because the majority of those in power are not motivated by a high ideal. Naturally, they would never be so stupid, so insane as to have such a sublime goal! They are only interested in what they can get out of the situation. But if some of them do decide to achieve this ideal come what may, then, believe me, they will find true power, true light and true beauty.

The sad thing is that a great many adolescents do have this

desire to work for an ideal, to make great sacrifices, to conduct themselves as true, valiant knights. But then, after a time, when they come up against hard facts and are urged by those around them to be 'sensible' and 'realistic', they abandon their dreams and try to adapt and become like others. Obviously, even if a person's aspirations and impulses are excellent, he needs support; he needs someone to advise him and help him not to go back on the choices he has made, otherwise he will be worn down by a multitude of little difficulties and the jokes and jeers of his companions until he becomes exactly like the wild beasts all round him.

When I talk about the aristocracy, therefore, I am talking about the true inner aristocracy. When this aristocracy succeeds in maintaining its pre-eminent position in a human being, harmony reigns amongst the whole population of cells but, if it is unequal to its task, it is overthrown and its opponents — his instincts, lusts, vices and failings — take power into their own hands. And then, as the revolutionary song has it, all the aristocrats will be strung up! This always happens when the inner nobility is unworthy: the aristocrats are sent to the guillotine and the rabble takes power into its own hands.

And, very often, this is what happens to you, too. Of course, the blind won't see it but, if you meet an Initiate, he will understand the situation immediately and will say, 'My poor fellow, why on earth have you let things degenerate to such an extent? You're no better than a slave! And you don't even know how it happened! Well, it is for one of three reasons: either you lacked light, or you had no love for the divine world, or you didn't have the will-power to keep working.' There are only three possible explanations, not four or five or ten or more. People always see the causes of their misfortune outside themselves: their parents, society, their education, a shortage of money, the ill-will of neighbours, competitors, etc., etc. No, it is simply a lack of intelligence, love or will-power. This is how an Initiate envisages things. He knows that it is no good looking for causes in the external world; they must be sought in a person's inner life. Human beings are going to have to adopt entirely new criteria if they are to see the true causes of what happens to them.

When I talked to you about Agharta[1], I particularly emphasised the nature of its government: an aristocracy whose orders are always respected and obeyed by the whole population for it has never failed in its duty. And this is the form of government that must, one day, be established on earth. This idea may not be to the liking of some; they may have other convictions and other plans, but that is not my business; my business is simply to tell you how things should be.

But, first and foremost, it is within yourselves that the aristocracy must be reinstated. You must cherish and protect all that is noble, pure and luminous in your own being. This is just what an Initiate is: someone who is always alert to protect the divine faculties within him. Unfortunately, most human beings never think about protecting their inner aristocracy. In exchange for a part in a film, a photograph in a magazine or the promise of fine clothes and jewellery, a charming young girl will willingly shed all her freshness and purity. In exchange for fabulous sums of money, a scientist will put all his exceptional intelligence and skills at the service of destructive forces. Is this the way to protect and safeguard one's inner aristocracy? Far from it; this is the way to betray and overthrow it and trample it underfoot. Nothing in the world, no amount of money, no promise of fame or glory would ever persuade an Initiate to betray his aristocracy. He knows that it is thanks to this aristocracy of wise, luminous, intelligent beings within him that he will, one day, be in a position to call heaven and earth his own. No one can offer him anything remotely comparable to this.

When will human beings make up their minds to stop putting their most precious gifts and qualities at the service of Hell?

Sèvres, February 1, 1976

1 See the last lecture in this volume.

Chapter Eight

Politics in the Light of Initiatic Science

I

In the talk we have just listened to[1], I said that evolution was accompanied by a simplification of forms and an amplification of the intensity of life, whereas involution was accompanied by a multiplication of forms and a diminution in the intensity of life, a loss of expressiveness, subtlety and refinement. This is why, when man debases himself, he sinks more deeply into diversity and becomes a world teeming with savage, snarling beasts — snakes, crocodiles, tigers and jackals. This is because man's inner life is simply the reflection of his outer life; when he moves further from the Source, he reproduces within himself the conditions of the jungle and is torn by inner conflict and strife. The only way he can put an end to this unhappy situation is to turn back to unity.

This unity must also be established amongst the countries of the world. Study your history books and you will see that, not so very long ago, many of the existing countries were split up into separate, warring States. Eventually, these small States realized that it would be to their advantage to unite and, in doing so, they have become world powers. But this is only one stage in the

1 This lecture is a commentary on one that is published in *Complete Works*, vol. 17, 'Jnana-Yoga', chap. 9.

process; it is not enough. Each of these powers feels threatened by — and is a threat to — its neighbours, and the final outcome of the war they are preparing can only be their mutual destruction. Human beings must realize that the time has come to achieve a much broader, more all-embracing unity: every country in the world must unite, and that unification will produce in the body of the world exactly what it produces in our own bodies: health, strength and well-being. Mankind has not yet reached a satisfactory state of health; it is ill, suffering from cancer, because of the all-pervading philosophy of separativeness. Each individual wants to work only for his own country or his own family. But this tendency can only create an everlasting series of complications and wars because, in such divisive conditions, there will always be some whose interests are overlooked. It is time, now, to simplify things, to convince all the countries of the world that, if they agree to unite, they will be much better off: everyone will share in the new abundance and be free to travel, get to know other people and rejoice together.

In the past, of course, these notions of separativeness were perfectly normal; they had a role to play for man was not capable of broadening the scope of his consciousness to any great extent. Even the great Initiates such as Moses, for example, encouraged their people in the idea that they had to combat foreign nations; in fact, Moses himself participated in such wars. At that period it was impossible to get human beings to understand brotherly love and the need for a universal family. They were too much like animals; the thing was unthinkable. But the situation is no longer the same and, thanks to the speed of communications, the world has suddenly grown so small that the time has come for human beings to understand that they must do away with the barriers between countries and unite so that the whole world may be one immense family. Human beings are still fighting, but what are they defending? They are defending a state of affairs which is destined to disappear and, one day, they will realize how stupid they were to work so hard to preserve it.

In the meantime, however, they cling to their old political and religious conceptions. Christians, for example, continue to take pride in belonging to the true religion, in being the true children of God; they consider that all others are pagans, infidels, unbelievers. But this is grotesque, ridiculous, absolutely monstrous! True children of God cannot be so narrow-minded. As long as this is their attitude, they are on a very low level — and it is not I who put them on that level, it is they themselves. Every creature decides his own level and his own orientation by entertaining thoughts, feelings and acts which put him in contact with specific substances, regions and forces in the universe. Every day, at each instant of the day, we ally ourselves with good or with evil, with the light or with darkness.

It is visible that a tremendous work is going on, today, and it will be carried on with increasing intensity, if not by adults, then by the young. For it is the young who will find it impossible to endorse the obsolete conceptions that are the cause of all wars and who will force adults to see things from a broader perspective. Young people are coming to the fore; they are going to turn the world upside down in Russia as well as in America; they will bring about a tremendous revolution. Political leaders too often imagine that the destiny of a country is in their hands. They may be able to comfort themselves with this illusion for a time, but not for long. All those who have believed that everything depended on them, have come to a bad end. Tyrants always come to a bad end; they cut off a few heads but, in the end, others come along and then it is their turn to lose their heads. In reality, the destiny of mankind is not ruled by human beings, however mighty, but by very exalted Entities who watch over the world and control the course of events.

Think of all those mighty empires that once subjugated the world: they have all disappeared and been replaced by others. Yes, there are other intelligences, other forces working towards a goal that is unknown to us. Human beings should be much humbler, therefore, otherwise they are bound, sooner or later, to bite the dust. None of the innumerable secret societies that once believed they were going to rule the world has ever succeeded, and most of them have ceased to exist. Whereas the great Initiates, those who serve God's design, although they have often been scorned and massacred, have kept their ideal intact. For God's design is always the salvation, liberation and happiness of mankind.

My dear brothers and sisters, the Universal White Brotherhood exists to remind human beings that they are children of the same Father and the same Mother. Why should they slaughter each other? Why should they work against each other? It is monstrous, insane! You are obliged to agree with this conclusion: once you accept this truth you cannot continue to be separate and to detest each other, it's illogical. You must either live according to this truth or you should reject it — it would be more honest. Perhaps, if people had neither the same father nor the same mother, it would be permissible to massacre each other, but to behave like the Christians, who profess to believe that we are all children of the same Father and Mother, and who continue, in spite of that, to massacre Christians and non-Christians alike. Such a thing simply should not be. It is a terrible contradiction!

Human beings seek happiness, success and wealth for themselves and are always ready to spring to the defence of these things, believing that, if they don't, they will lose them. Only thirty years ago, the Frenchman who dared to suggest that his people should seek reconciliation with the Germans would have been shot. And now that the idea is accepted, neither the French nor the Germans are in danger of being shot for making friends, visiting each other — and even bringing a few little Franco-Germans into the world! Why shouldn't it be the same with all the other nations? The fact that the French and Germans are friends has not really changed things very much; they still have other enemies who are just waiting for the chance to devour them. If we are really to be out of danger, therefore, the unity we need must be much broader in scope. Otherwise, neither arms nor diplomacy will be capable of saving poor, suffering humanity. But the day will come when the dangers that threaten men will be so great that they will be forced to be friends. Yes, even the United States and Vietnam, even Israel and the Arab countries.

The only way for human beings to solve their problems is to live a brotherly life, and this is the life that I am offering them, a life which will give them an expanded consciousness and greater intelligence, happiness and joy. But the poor things cannot see this. The Brotherhood opens vast horizons to them; it offers them a family and immense wealth, but they refuse to leave their own little burrow, their egoism and darkness, their problems and their agony, because they continue to be ruled by their lower nature. They say, 'I don't need a Brotherhood; I don't need to learn any of that; all I want is to live my life freely and independently.' In reality, what they are defending in this way is their sloth and egoism, a wanton, undisciplined way of life, because that is what suits them.

The trouble is that human beings have no real touchstone by which to guide themselves; they are still babies. If they were adult — spiritually adult — they would recognize that it is their predilection for comfort and facility, their desire to 'enjoy' life that is the source of all misfortunes. But, as they have never analysed themselves, they still prefer this attitude, because it dispenses them from making an effort or trying to improve. Well, I must warn them that, as long as they have this attitude, they will never make any progress because they are behaving like children. Children always prefer something agreeable, pleasant, sweet; their intelligence is not sufficiently developed for them to understand that the sweet things of life won't help them to evolve. Sometimes, in order to develop and become strong and intelligent, we have to accept something bitter, some quinine. Some people have even sought martyrdom deliberately, because they knew that human beings evolved more rapidly in difficult conditions. To be sure, I am not going to ask you to go to such lengths, but I do ask you to understand that you must break with this philosophy of separativeness that so many people adopt in order to be, as they think, free and independent. You will never be free that way; on the contrary, you will be slaves, slaves to your own whims and weaknesses.

True development can only take place in a collectivity. When you are always alone there is nothing to make you control yourself or help others. You can sleep all day, go unwashed and live in squalor and disorder. Some people prefer to live in sordid conditions; they feel comfortable that way, but in a collectivity it would be frightful! You have to be clean and presentable so as not to be offensive to others; you have to be friendly, patient and tolerant. Some people tell me that they need to be alone because they have so much work to do. Come on now! Don't think you can fool me so easily: I can see the reflection of that 'work' in their faces, and it is nothing but laziness, pleasure, the life of the astral plane or of even lower, subterranean regions in which they spend their time raising the dust and stirring up the mud and the tadpoles. But one fine day they are going to wake up to the fact that they are completely enslaved, that they have been working for their enemies, for entities of darkness they don't even know. It is these entities that order them about: 'Get me this or that to eat. No, I don't like that; go and get me the other thing, etc.' And they are forever running about, trying to satisfy what they take to be their own desires. Yes, and this state of affairs will continue until they finally realize that they have compromised their future and their own happiness by feeding and pandering to their worst enemies.

You must be aware that every human being is inhabited by two types of entity, and if they don't know which ones to nourish, they end by being completely dominated by the entities of darkness. In order to milk them to the last drop, to get the last scrap of meat off them, these entities tell them, 'You're free! You can do what you please', and the poor fools are convinced that they have been 'liberated' as they would say. They don't realize that, on the contrary, they have been enslaved. Man can be free, but not by surrendering to all his desires. As long as people understand freedom in the manner of children, they will never know liberty, only slavery.

Do as you please, therefore, but, sooner or later, you will be obliged to arrive at the same truths that I am giving you today. And the sooner you get there the better! You have already had so many costly experiences, is there any point in going on in the same way? Couldn't you find a better kind of experience? I am continually astonished by people's mentality: they say, 'But its important to sample all kinds of experiences'. I agree. Absolutely. But why do you experiment only with dark, negative things? You must at least be honest about it, and if you insist on sampling everything, then you must also sample luminous, spiritual things. If you really feel that you must try everything, why limit yourself to only one aspect?

Man, unfortunately, always concentrates on one side of things – usually the worst side – and neglects the other. When a philosopher – a self-styled philosopher – declares that there is nothing in life for man but emptiness and despair, that God does not exist or that, if He does, man has no way of communicating with Him, the masses rush to follow him. And yet, even if there is an element of truth in that point of view, wouldn't it be equally true to say the exact opposite? Why do human beings confine themselves to one aspect – and always the worst? There are always two sides to everything and you must look at both. A human being has two natures, one that is celestial and the other that is infernal, and you must study both of them. Yes, but you must give first place to his celestial nature.

Now, have you really understood what I have been saying? Have you understood that the Universal White Brotherhood is a truly terrible place, as unpleasant, indigestible and tough as can be? If you have understood this, then you will come here to practise and get into training, to develop to the full every aspect of your being – will, heart, intellect, soul and spirit – and, one day, you will become true sons and daughters of God.

God is above all considerations of race or nationality. He has not created human beings to be Jews, Arabs, Christians or Buddhists: He has created them; that's all. It is they who, because of the conditions in which they evolved, were obliged to form clans, families, societies and nations. One day these distinctions which lead to so much hostility will disappear and men will feel themselves to be citizens of the world. Isn't this the healthiest and most desirable thing we could possibly wish for? Where is the political leader who would contradict me? I can demonstrate to you, mathematically, scientifically and historically, that certain points of view are obsolete.

Now that we are living in an age in which man has reached the moon, isn't it about time we decided to change certain things? One fine day we shall meet the inhabitants of the moon. You will tell me that science has discovered that there are no inhabitants on the moon. But there are! In fact, they are more scientifically and technologically advanced than man. Why did the astronauts find no sign of them? Because, knowing in advance that they were going to have visitors, they hid away in their underground homes. Yes, because, if human beings are capable of reaching the moon, they are also perfectly capable, sooner or later, of doing to its inhabitants what the Spanish did to the Aztecs and Mayas. They still do it, wherever they go; there's not much difference, in fact, between cannibals and so-called civilized people. If they don't actually eat their fellow men, they devour them in other ways. Ah, I know that you like cannibals... shall I tell you a story about them?

One day a delegation of cannibals turned up at the United Nations, saying, 'We demand a hearing; we have some complaints to make. We have learned from the newspapers and television (as you see, cannibals are very civilized and up-to-date) that you help people who are starving. You send them supplies of wheat, rice and coffee, etc., but you have sent us only a dozen missionaries. That's not enough; we ate the last of them a long time ago and now we're hungry. Why can't you apply a little Christian generosity to our case, too!' How logical! You will say, of course, 'But human beings learned not to eat each other a long time ago!' Oh, you know, there are many cases to prove that the twentieth century is not really so far removed from cannibalism. Put human beings in certain situations and you will see how highly evolved they are. Besides, to eat someone is no worse than all the other things people do. No one has yet studied all the various forms of cannibalism such as the different ways in which men and women 'eat' each other.

Let people do as they please; let them swindle and destroy, if they want to, but they must never forget that it is not they who control the situation. There are other entities, above us, who watch over mankind and guide it in its evolution. Some men and women have devoted sixty, seventy, even eighty years to studying the will of their superior — the boss, the general or the minister — but these are purely human wills and they have wasted their time. I have devoted my whole life to studying the will of God and now I know it. And you, too, can know it.

And now, my dear brothers and sisters, remember all this and think about what I said in the beginning about simplicity and complication. By moving away from simplicity and unity and towards diversity, men's spirits sank into the realm of the roots, and roots live in the darkness and cold of the subterranean world. It is time, now, to climb back up into warmth and light, into the realm of the flowers. And in flowers, too, they will find quantities of different forms, colours and scents.

When you move away from the sun, everything is cold and dark and life diminishes. When you get closer to the sun, there is more light, more warmth and more life. In the same way, those who move away from God have no more warmth, no love, no light, no wisdom and no life: they become crystallized. This is why they are incapable of understanding or feeling, incapable, even, of doing anything. Or, if they do succeed in doing something, it is always destructive. But those who, like the Initiates, have turned back towards the Deity, are again blessed with

light, warmth and life and they accomplish marvels, even to
the point of raising the dead. It is so simple; even children can
understand. So why can't the philosophers? If they understood
they would not stray so far from the Source. Do you imagine
that what people read in books nowadays helps them to get closer
to the Source? No, there is too much that is negative in books,
too many elements that are destructive of faith, love and morals,
that demolish all sense of the sacred and the divine. You must
read other books or, rather, you must read the only book that
is really worthwhile: the book of nature. And you must get ever
closer to the spiritual sun so as to be warmed, illuminated and
vivified.

Unfortunately, human beings do just the opposite: they do
all they can to get further away and nothing to get closer. And
then you hear them say, 'I don't understand what's happening;
I don't know where I stand any more'. Certainly, to say this does
not speak well for anyone and yet I have heard it or read it in
the letters of quantities of people. I have always answered these
people kindly so as not to offend them but, if I had given them
my true diagnosis, I would have said, 'I'm not surprised that you
don't understand what's happening to you. In fact, you will
understand less and less, because you are going in the wrong direction!' Then there are those who complain that they can't bear
other people; they just don't love others. And my diagnosis of
what ails them is no better: it is as though they handed me their
identity card on which I read, 'I'm an idiot, an imbecile, a
monster!' The printing on the card actually reads, 'Doctor So-
and-so, Professor Such-and-such, Minister of this-or-that' but
what I see is quite different: it says, 'Imbecile'. Why? Because
they are incapable of loving others. Can you imagine! And whom
do they love? Themselves, of course, and even then they do it
very badly. Then, again, there are those who say, 'I don't seem
to be able to make an effort any more; I'm weak, paralysed'.
What has brought them to such a state of weakness? The fact
that they have surrendered to the inferior beings who inhabit them

and who have bound them hand and foot so that, now, they are helpless. This, too, is a terrible thing to have on one's identity card.

There, this is how I understand things and, if you wish, you can come to understand them in the same way. If you do, it will be all the better for you, for no one will ever be able to mislead you again; no one! I shall give you the yardsticks, the criteria you need and you will be able to look at someone and say, 'My friend, you can't fool me any longer; it's too late. I see through you!' But begin by using these yardsticks and criteria for yourself, first of all. There is no hurry about applying them to others; we can see about that later.

Sèvres, February 18, 1968

II

I know that when people who keep abreast of what is going on in the world listen to my lectures they find that the things I talk about have no connection with current events. They say, 'What on earth is he talking about? If he knew what was going on in Spain or Portugal or the Lebanon — even in France — he wouldn't waste his time talking about such insignificant things.' Well, this remark only shows how little they understand, for what I am giving you is, on the contrary, the foundation of all the rest. What I give you are the methods, means and keys you need to solve all of life's problems.

What good would it do if I talked to you about world events? There are already so many people who do that, but they never have any solutions to offer. All they do is reel off statistics and make statements and reports which are no use to anyone. Besides, the Lord alone knows if they are accurate! So, for my part, I leave all those questions to others and concern myself with essentials, with things that will be valid for all eternity. Human beings have a physical body, a will, a heart, an intellect, a soul and a spirit, and the great question is to see how he must work with these elements which will always be part of him. Yes, for the rest of eternity, whatever else may occur in the world, every human being is going to be faced with the same problems: how to think, feel, act, love and create.

The subject I choose to talk about, therefore, is the one most important subject there is: human beings. Other people don't see the importance of this; they waste their time and energy on things that will soon be forgotten. I am always amazed to see how human beings have this tendency to be fascinated by trivialities. A new government, for instance, gets them all worked up, but how long is that government going to last? A few months later it will be changed and they will have to switch their attention to the next one! As for political parties, they come and go and change their names, and if you don't know their names or who their leaders are, everybody looks down on you! No one minds if you know nothing about the divine world, that is unimportant, but not to know the names of party leaders, not to know what their latest squabbles are about, what they said to each other on television, etc., that is disgraceful! How petty and pathetic it all is! What can any of that contribute to the real future of human beings, that is to say, to their peace, light and immortality?

You will say, 'But people are interested in politics because they want to help the country'. I know, but that is not the way to help it; no one has ever helped humanity in that way. They are deluding themselves if they think that all these political discussions and dissensions are capable of helping humanity, because they are not. They have never produced anything but discontent, anger, strikes and revolutions. What has ever been improved by politics? Hospitals are overflowing, criminal cases flood the courts and we shall soon need one policeman for every inhabitant. I shall show you, one day, through the power of our Teaching, that there are other means that we can use to solve all these problems.

You will find thousands of people in the world who think that politics takes priority over everything else. But, although they think of nothing else, day and night, what solutions have they ever found? None, except to belong to a party. Ah, that is important; it is a great feather in your cap to belong to a political

party! But does that party hold the solutions to the world's problems? Does it have the right philosophy, the right outlook?
Nobody asks themselves that. Once they are members of a party, they feel strong and secure and self-complacent. Yes, but their
complacency may not last long; if their party is beaten at the polls
they are going to be completely deflated. Their glory was nothing
but a soap bubble!

Do you agree with me? No, I don't think you do! Well, have it
your own way, but let me tell you that as long as the synarchy is
not established, it is no good counting on any of the myriad forms
of anarchy. Believe me, all the different tendencies manifesting
themselves today are, to a greater or a lesser degree, tendencies towards anarchy. Of course, I know that the French will not approve
of me if I say this; if only they could realize how far they are from
the truth! The fact is that they like being mistaken, they enjoy
their illusions, they like having something to do even if it serves
no useful purpose. At least they keep busy; they're not idle;
they're doing something to kill time. True, it is good to be active, but they could, at least, choose the best kind of activity.

If you start talking about politics in public, in the street or
in a train, for instance, you will find that everybody, young and
old alike, is ready to voice brilliant political ideas. But, Heavens
above, their lives are so restricted and so bound up in their personality, what ideas can they possibly have? And if you listen
to the leaders of the political parties, you will hear each of them
in turn accusing the others of working for the ruin of the nation
and the grief of its citizens, whereas he, of course, is selflessly
devoted to his country! Is all this sincere? Are they really talking about the interests of the country and their fellow citizens
or are they seeking their own interest, hoping to be elected for
their own sakes? Once they are elected, of course, the truth will
out! And, unfortunately, that truth will simply be 'more of the
same'. It is because people cannot agree about what constitutes
'the good of the country' that there are so many political parties: new parties crop up every day. We need to seek an overall

view, a view of the unique, ultimate goal; this is something that has never been found or even envisaged. Instead of fixing our sights on a unique and final goal, each individual focuses on one particular aspect and is ready to do battle in defence of a partial, temporary ideal which will soon be replaced by something else. For great upheavals are on the way and human beings will be obliged to understand that their vision of reality was distorted. The Invisible World, of course, knows this; that is why these upheavals will be permitted: for the good of mankind.

I am not saying that everybody is completely wrong; no, each one sees things correctly from his own point of view. But they are all mistaken in respect to the whole. An egoist, who pays no attention to other people's interests, arranges things in such a way as to satisfy his own appetites and desires. Inevitably, others rebuke him for this but he cannot understand their criticism because, from his own point of view, what he is doing is perfectly reasonable, logical and legitimate. And this is exactly what happens with political parties. What they say is all perfectly true and logical from their point of view, but when seen from a universal point of view, from the point of view of the whole, it is not quite so true!

When a child wants to do something he is convinced that it is only normal and right and he gets a nasty shock when his parents forbid it or punish him for doing it. From his point of view, with the degree of understanding that is his, what he wants seems to be logical and legitimate, so he is furious with anyone who stands in his way and refuses to let him do what he wants; he thinks that they are both wicked and stupid. And this is exactly what happens in the world. Everybody tries to impose his will on others: 'To my mind it's like this' and 'to my mind it's like that'. Yes, but 'your mind' is terribly limited! What we need is to broaden the scope of our minds and become capable of seeing things not only from our own personal point of view and according to our own needs and wishes, but from other people's point of view too, and of using their point of view to modify or complete our own.

Only when we do this shall we discover the truth and realize that everybody is both right and wrong: that is to say that they are all right from their own point of view, but not from the point of view of the cosmic collectivity.

As long as man is not sufficiently broad-minded, impersonal and highly evolved, he can only see things from his own point of view and his 'personal truth' will be only a fragment of the whole truth. Political parties are necessarily in error, therefore, for they all see things only from their own point of view. When they begin to see reality as it truly is they will be less proud of their original ideology. For my part, I try to see things not only from my own point of view but from the point of view of those who are more advanced, and this explains why my view of things is true. Those who make no effort to cultivate this higher point of view are bound to get things wrong and, sooner or later, life itself will prove it to them.

I am not opposed to politics, but I understand it differently. If power is in the hands of someone who knows nothing about the structure of man or his links with all the different powers of the cosmos, how can you expect him to do anything really good for his country? If he has not done so for himself, how can he do so for a whole nation? How can a fool instruct others? How can a weakling bear other people's burdens? How can someone who is impure purify others? It's impossible! And it is also impossible for politicians to bring happiness to their people if they have never been instructed in an Initiatic school, for only in such a school can they learn that, before anyone can be a true political leader, he must have a profound knowledge of man and nature and a profound respect for divine law. Also, he must be free from all ambition, all personal passions.

Everyone talks about serving his country but that is often nothing but words; they are mainly interested in their pocket-books, their prestige and their power, and are ready to fight their way to the top with hoof and claw and nail. The rare few who are more enlightened but who are not prepared to fight tooth and nail to get to the top are ignored. As I say, I am not against politics, but for me the only valid form of politics is that of the Initiates who have studied human nature and know all its strengths and weaknesses, who know what it needs and what spiritual, emotional, moral and economic conditions are most conducive to its fulfilment. As long as this knowledge is lacking, politics can only lead to conflict.

Even Karl Marx, who is so revered and appreciated, who has so many faithful followers — even he will lose all prestige before long, and all his acolytes with him! Yes, because the problems of humanity cannot all be resolved by class warfare and the collective ownership of the means of production, etc. I am not saying that Marx was not a genius; he was. You can't deny it. But nor can anyone deny that he could not foresee everything, that he did not live a divine life and that he was not an Initiate. I realize, of course, that we need people who are qualified in every aspect of social and economic life, but most important of all, we need the leadership of Initiates who may know nothing about these specific problems but who understand the essentials.

Does this astonish you? Take my case, for instance. No one on earth is as ignorant as I am about political organization, economics or finance. I know nothing about any of that! But one thing I do know, only one: how to keep the water flowing! That's all. And water can be relied on to find its own channels and to make it possible for a whole culture to spring up and develop: plants, animals and men. The important thing is to keep the water coming and not to bother about the rest. And that is what I do: my work is to keep the water flowing and then you — like the plants, birds, trees and animals that form a community at the site of a spring — each one of you can find your own niche. It is not up to me to find a place for you; that is not my job. In fact, that is why I have absolutely no talent for organization. My only care is to ensure that there is plenty of water, for where there is water, the rest takes care of itself. And water is love: love and life!

As long as economists and politicians forget about the need for water and think that all they have to do to improve the situation is set up a good organization, create new institutions and new structures or new administrative posts, the process of death and disintegration will continue. Whatever is done on the purely external, organizational level will be ineffectual if nothing is done to ensure the flow of water. This is why it is essential that there should be someone at the top who is rich in light, knowledge and love, for then every branch and every department will know how to contribute to the success of the whole.

You can see this phenomenon so clearly in your own life. Perhaps you don't know exactly how to set about whatever it is you have to do, but you love it, you love your work, and in this case you will succeed and do it very well, because love always finds a way. But if you don't love it, you will never be any good at it, however hard you try. Some women, for instance, read all kinds of cookbooks and use all the best ingredients, but the meals they turn out are inedible. Why? Because they hate cooking! And then there are others who never read a cookbook and who manage, no one quite knows how, to turn out delicious meals with the most ordinary ingredients. The answer is simple: they love doing it. It's a question of love. Of course, I am not a child: I know that the organization involved in running a country is extremely complex. Yes, but if everything is to run smoothly there must be light, there must be love, there must be water. When the flow of water is assured everyone receives the inspiration he needs to find his own special role.

Look what happens when a group of people meet to discuss a joint project. If the members of the group love each other it will be much easier for them to understand each other, and by the end of the meeting, everything will have been settled and their plans will meet with success. But if they come to the meeting without love, in order to contradict, criticize and oppose the ideas of others, they will never find any solutions. This is what happens in many committees, simply because there is no love between the members. And here, in the Brotherhood, if some of you have never managed to settle certain problems satisfactorily, it is because you simply haven't understood the Teaching; I want to make this quite clear to you. For, when you are really inspired by love, it often takes just five minutes to resolve problems which, without love, will stay unresolved for years.

Why are human beings still so blind? And to think that they have such a high opinion of themselves! Believe me, if you are incapable of solving your problems, you have no cause to be so pleased with yourselves. If you are capable of solving them, alright; but, if not, you would do better to find a quiet spot in which to reflect on what it is in you that makes it impossible: your lack of love. The trouble is that people don't believe in the power of love. They only believe in the power of the intellect, in the power of a critical mind. For my part I have no faith in the effectiveness of such things; in fact, they are dangerous. Bring a little more love to the situation and your problems will be solved immediately and everyone will go their separate ways, happy and astonished that it was all so simple.

You must have seen two people discussing something: have you noticed how they both talk at the same time? No wonder they end by coming to blows! Yes, because they don't listen to each other. They are both so full of themselves that they are incapable of listening to anyone else, they get more and more irritated and impatient and lose their self-control to such an extent that they actually start to fight. Really, people have no psychology or pedagogical sense! If they had any intelligence at all they would know in advance what the outcome was liable to be and avoid reaching that point. An intelligent man begins by manifesting love and good-will and listens to what someone is saying to him; in this way he calls out the best in the other person and their problems can be resolved.

But, to get back to the question of politics: I assure you that, as long as political leaders are ignorant of Initiatic Science, they are bound to make mistakes. Of course, as the public has no yardstick by which to judge, they are full of admiration. They say, 'Did you hear how So-and-so put the other fellow down? Wasn't it splendid? He really blasted him; it was magnificent!' And all the ignorant fools are thrilled. Yes, but an Initiate who saw that would not be thrilled at all. With the blind, anything goes; they will swallow anything, but an Initiate will not be taken in. Whom do adolescents choose as heroes? Those who are violent and destructive, those who are quickest on the draw! And the masses are exactly like adolescents.

You must not expect much from politics, therefore, until political leaders have studied Initiatic Science; there will be more and more difficulties, conflicts and misunderstandings and they will be unable to find solutions. They think that they don't need the light of this science. Well, they will see whether they need it or not; there are some surprises in store for them that will force them to be more mature in their attitudes and then they will understand that this science is not to be scoffed at.

Yes, I have to tell you the truth even if some people don't like to hear it. As long as the truth about mankind, the universe and the Creator is unknown, any solutions that may be found will be only partial, makeshift and temporary; they cannot be perfect, they will always involve certain inconveniences. If Râma instituted a Golden Age during which mankind enjoyed centuries of peace and prosperity, it was because he had been instructed in Initiatic Science by a mysterious being who guided and advised him. Eventually, the light of that Science was lost and, once again, anarchy and violence took over and has reigned, now, for many thousands of years.

Today, it is neither moral qualities nor intelligence that has the upper hand, but force. Everybody wants power because everybody is persuaded that power, the use of force, is the surest way to achieve success. But let me tell you that it is the very worst way. Power must never be first; it must always be last. A synarchic form of government puts love, wisdom and truth in first place, and power and economic interests are seen as second-ary in importance. But, in today's world, this order is reversed: power and economics are given priority, and this is why the situ-ation is going from bad to worse and, whatever people may think, it will not right itself because this order is contrary to the laws of the cosmos, to the universal order.

The only type of organization that reflects the structure of the universe is a synarchy. All other systems of government are expressions of anarchy and this is why the world is in such dis-array. Men will never succeed in establishing peace and order in society if they continue to act in contradiction to the divine laws, in contradiction to the principles that govern the structure of the universe. It is impossible! I want to uproot these false notions from your minds. The Master Peter Deunov said to me one day, 'You are the great demolisher'. And what do I demolish? Your old, antiquated notions. And if there are still some who hope to succeed in life without the light and through the use of violence, let me demolish that hope once and for all: if they continue to cling to it, it will be their downfall. In fact, you will see this; everyone, beginning with themselves, will see it.

This is a lecture that could revolutionize men's consciousness. Yes, because light is the most powerful revolutionary force that exists. No force is more revolutionary than the light. Many highly evolved beings have avoided speaking about these things because they knew how narrow-minded and limited human beings were and how dangerous it would be to reveal truths that were so far beyond their grasp, so they refused to enlighten the masses. But the time has come, now, for the whole of mankind to know these truths.

So, let's concentrate on the heart of the matter. If a man refuses the Teaching of the Universal White Brotherhood, which reveals the existence of a higher but absolutely real world, he can never be a good head of State, because he will always be subject to impulses and ambitions dictated by self-interest, van-ity, a desire for revenge, etc., and, in these conditions he can

never make his people happy. To be sure, anybody can pull
the wool over people's eyes and prevent them from detect-
ing their true motives with well chosen words and gestures,
noble phrases and speeches about the safety of the father-
land, the happiness of its citizens, true justice, etc., etc.
But the reality? Well, the reality is not for public consumption: as you can well imagine, if they showed themselves
as they really were and made no secret of their lust, their will
for power and so on, no one would accept their leadership. They
know that. That is why they bluff and lie and pretend to be what
they are not.

In the past, men such as Genghis Khan, Attila and Tamerlane
could get what they wanted even though they showed themselves exactly as they were. But, in those days, the mentality
was not the same and the more unjust, cruel and pitiless a leader
showed himself to be, the better his chances of success. Whereas,
nowadays, you cannot do that; you have to show that your
goals are acceptable, reasonable, generous even, otherwise you
will be defeated. That is why people take great care to conceal
their fangs behind a show of good manners so as to attract their
victims and then... 'all the better to eat you with, my dear!'
Yes, because their victims are without intuition, without intelligence, without knowledge. With a little perseverance, you can
win over almost anyone, even by dishonest means, as long as
you don't show yourself as you really are.

If you want to find people who are absolutely disinterested,
you must turn to the great Initiates who have proved themselves,
who have purified themselves and endured great suffering, but
who have conquered and emerged victorious. No one else is
worthy of your trust. You can trust a man only if his higher nature
has triumphed over his lower nature, not otherwise. Otherwise,
whatever he may tell you, be on your guard! I don't ask you to
trust and believe me or to follow me. All I ask is that you come
and live with me for a while and see for yourself. If, when you
have spent months or years with me and seen how I live, you con-

clude that you can trust me, then you are free to follow me. But I have never told anyone to follow me from the very first day.

If you accept the Universal White Brotherhood, you need look no further; this is where you will find happiness. Surrounded by so many brothers and sisters, bombarded by so many loving looks and friendly smiles, how could you be anything but happy? But, if you prefer to be alone in your own little hole and to cling to your philosophy of universal isolation, you will never be happy. People think they will find happiness by isolating themselves, but happiness is impossible in isolation. Happiness is to be part of a collectivity; only when you are part of this universal brotherhood, of this immensity, can happiness slip into you... and it will never slip away from you again. All those poor wretches who continue to believe that they will find happiness by isolating themselves from others, by being selfish and personal... the only thing in store for them is death and disintegration.

Izgrev, December 27, 1975

III

Human beings don't really know what it is they are looking for and, when they have tried everything and still feel inwardly dissatisfied, they plunge headlong into all kinds of dangerous experiences hoping to escape from their stifling conditions of life. What they are really looking for is space, infinity, eternity, that nourishment for the soul and spirit that a materialistic philosophy has never allowed for. And this is why materialism is going to be defeated. Yes, certain events are going to take place and materialism will be no more.

There are some who try to make human beings believe that their happiness depends on technical progress and material comfort, and in doing so, they make it impossible for them to breathe, to be in contact with other regions and other entities which, alone, could give them the peace, love and fulfilment they need. The spiritual, mystical world has been so fiercely rejected, scorned and ridiculed that hardly anyone is tempted to turn to it for the elements he needs for survival. This is why mankind is dying of asphyxiation, of poisoning. Here, in the Brotherhood, it is just the opposite: you are given the best possible conditions to help you to be in communication with the subtle world and breathe, eat and drink of it to your heart's content. And yet, you don't actually receive anything material. When you are meditating you are not being given any food or drink or perfume — nothing. And in this nothingness your soul finds fulfilment.

If human beings don't make up their minds to take the path of spirituality they will inevitably deteriorate, for no one can survive by absorbing only what is contrary to his nature. As I have always said, man does not know himself; even science doesn't know him; it knows nothing about where man comes from, where he is going, what he should do or his need to be in communication with the spiritual world. And this is why human beings are constantly assaulted, despoiled and ill-treated: because their true nature is never taken into consideration. And this has always gone on, in every area of life.

You only have to think of how marriages were decided in the old days: parents obliged their daughter to marry the man of their choice, even if she had absolutely no feeling of affinity with him. She was obliged to sacrifice herself almost to the point of death in order to please them. This situation lasted for centuries until, one fine day, the pendulum swung back and, today, it has reached the opposite extreme: not only have young people stopped listening to their parents' advice, but parents are often the last to learn that their children are married and already have children of their own. In the past it was parents who exaggerated and, now, it is the children who exaggerate in the opposite direction.

For centuries, the Church tried to impose puritanical rules of behaviour on the faithful, and now, in recent years, we have begun to see the reaction: people are plunging impetuously and without inhibition into every cesspool they can find. And the same reaction is at work on the level of needs: adults have tried to force a purely material way of life on the young and to convince them that the only things that mattered were profits, production and consumption, with the result that they now feel impelled to escape from this materialism and find something different. And their need for diversion and escape often leads to drugs.

How many, many changes, even revolutions, human beings have experienced! But the situation has never really improved.

Why not? Because, in spite of their revolutions, people have never been able to break out of the vicious circle of their lower desires and ambitions. Until there is a real improvement in mentalities, conditions will never be any better. You must break free from these lower regions of appetites and lusts; only then will the changes you introduce be an improvement. If you don't change the materials, the elements, the ingredients you work with, however many different ways you find to combine them, you will still be working in the lower regions where all is dark, cold and lifeless. You must rise to a higher level where all is light, space and purity.

The Roman populace clamoured for bread and games, and this well-known incident in Roman history is often mentioned as though no other people in the world had ever made similar demands. The fact is that human beings still clamour for the same things even if the form they take is different. Their demands have been modernized, that's all; but people still want the same things: food and entertainment. Isn't this what strikes and revolutions are about: higher wages, shorter working hours, more leisure time? Of course, nobody asks for the Roman circus any more but, today, the circus has been replaced by the cinema, television, variety shows, night clubs, football, wrestling, etc. There is no lack of entertainment! Man's nature is still the same; it still hungers to be entertained, and a great variety of 'foods' has been found to satisfy its hunger. But how many people hunger for the Kingdom of God and His Righteousness? Does anyone demand light, purity, truth or kindness? No, the centre of interest is always money, food and pleasure.

The only thing of a spiritual nature for which human beings clamour is freedom, and freedom as they understand it boils down to having more opportunities to waste their time, amuse themselves and degrade themselves and others by indulging all their most insane whims. How many want to be free in order to devote their time to sublime activities? All political and social conflict turns on men's bellies and sexual appetites and their lust for money and pleasure. And this means that, if you give people what they clamour for, they will only become more deeply mired in their follies and passions.

Human beings have two natures, a lower nature, that we call the personality, and a higher nature, that we call the individuality. When a man's higher nature is in command, he is a divinity and is capable of doing immense good throughout the world. Whereas, if his personality is in command, it is far too self-centred and grasping to do anything good; it tries to turn everything to its own advantage; everybody has to subordinate their own interests and bow to its will, for it takes itself for the centre of the universe. Unfortunately, it is the personality that is in command everywhere and in everyone: in families, where we see husband and wife both trying to dominate the other; in society, where everyone tries to get ahead at the expense of others. Wherever you look, you see only personalities vociferating, threatening, giving orders... but human beings don't possess the criteria that would enable them to analyse themselves and understand why they feel the need to clamour for certain things or where this need comes from.

Only the sages, Initiates and great Masters, who trained their personality to be their servant, have been capable of manifesting their divine nature and leaving behind them an unforgettable, eternal, imperishable achievement. Such beings have always existed − history has preserved their memory − but they are very few compared to all the rampant personalities which people the earth, giving free rein to their lowest instincts of greed, hostility and revenge. Is there any wonder that the population suffers when people like this hold responsible positions in the political organization of a country? This is why there will never be an end to war: because of this philosophy of the personality. As long as a politician works to achieve his own ambitions or that of his party or even that of his country, he will inevitably commit many injustices. As long as everybody continues to practise the politics of the personality, the situation will never really improve: there will always be war and misery somewhere in the world. One day, someone must come and, at last, inaugurate the politics of the individuality.

A purely human practice of politics based on selfishness, guile and injustice is not true politics. But who is capable of governing according to true politics? How can someone who is ignorant work for the politics of enlightenment? He will let himself be led astray by those who are ready to fight tooth and nail for their privileges, and will not even see where they are leading him. There are millions of blind, gullible people ready and waiting to be hoodwinked and, as you can well imagine, there are always plenty of people willing to oblige them!

A great deal of knowledge is necessary in order to work in the political arena, knowledge that even politicians don't possess. In order to be elected, they promise voters everything imaginable, but, once they have won their seat, there is not really much they can do; their powers are very limited and they learn that it is not so easy as they thought. For my part, I think that it is the seat that is the cause of all their difficulties; they should never occupy the same seat as their predecessors, for each seat has a memory. Each seat is impregnated by the influences and emanations of all those who have occupied it and who have never fulfilled their promises and, in this way, each new occupant is necessarily affected by these influences. Yes, it is obviously the seat that is at fault. Don't laugh! As you see, I can find an explanation for everything.

If the Kingdom of God has not yet been established on earth it is because people work only for political goals dictated by their personality. When I analyse the aims of politicians, I find that they are uniformly mediocre. Oh, of course, they are dressed up and painted in bright colours to dazzle the public, but a closer look shows you that they all boil down to the same thing: 'Move over and make room for me!' They are all the same! But, little by little, people will realize that you cannot make a violin with a bit of old lumber; you have to find the right kind of wood.

Yes, politicians must be prepared and instructed in Initiatic schools, otherwise they will continue to lead the nations to disaster.

Does anyone ever think to scratch the surface and try to discover the secret ambitions that motivate those who wave flags and make high-flown speeches? No, they dash off to listen to them and are swept off their feet and follow them with enthusiasm. If only they could see what wolves, what wild boars are behind that smooth facade! But they see none of that; they have no judgement, no intuitive sense. It is a case of the blind leading the blind, and you know what the Gospel says: 'If the blind leads the blind, both will fall into a ditch.' Unfortunately, it is only years later that people realize that their blindness has led to catastrophe. Look at Hitler and Stalin and a host of others: they were monsters, murderers — and yet people acclaimed them and flocked to them!

I too am working for a political goal, but for one that is not inspired by my personality. It is sad that there are still so few people ready to understand these ideas. Try talking to them about a policy inspired by the individuality, a policy of generosity, disinterestedness and light: no one would take you seriously. But talk to them about destruction and arson, and thousands of people will enthusiastically agree. This is why — forgive me for saying this — but this is why human beings still need to suffer. No other explanation is possible: they still need to suffer and, one day, through suffering, they will find the way. You think that I am being cruel in saying this but, I assure you, although it gives me great pain to say it, it is true: human beings still need to suffer before they are ready to understand. If you need proof of this, just look at how they behave when a messenger from Heaven comes to instruct and help them: do they listen to him? Not a bit of it! Not only do they refuse to listen to him, but they imprison or crucify him or send him to the stake. But when a monster who is bound to bring them suffering comes along, they welcome him with open arms, acclaim him as their saviour and give him all the powers he needs to destroy them. Isn't it obvious that human beings need to suffer? They go looking for suffering.

But let's get back to this question of the personality and the individuality. The annals of Initiatic Science tell us that many human civilizations have already been wiped out and that the culture and technical skills of some of these civilizations – the Atlanteans, for instance – were far more advanced than ours. If they disappeared it was because of this perpetual tendency of the personality that drives people to try to dominate and subjugate others by force.

Unfortunately, this tendency is becoming more and more evident in the modern world and this bodes ill for the future of humanity. Wherever you look you see nations or political factions intent on dominating and crushing others, and increasingly lethal arms are being manufactured in ever greater quantities. If there is one type of industry which is never short of work it is the arms industry. Every country manufactures arms for themselves and for sale to others and, today, Africa is stocked with arms bought from other countries who, apparently, have never paused to consider that it will be they who suffer the consequences. This is what the human personality leads to. And this is why human beings must be instructed in the Teaching of the Universal White Brotherhood and shown how to use the tendencies of their personality in the service of their individuality. Yes, if mankind is to be saved, this light needs to be propagated throughout the world. Otherwise you may be sure that Cosmic Intelligence, Who dwells in eternity, is not likely to be unduly concerned about the disappearance of one more human race. So many others have already disappeared that if this one goes the same way through its own fault it will not trouble Cosmic Intelligence at all; It will simply use the few surviving individuals to start all over again. It is up to us not to destroy ourselves. If we persist in doing everything we can to bring destruction upon ourselves, Cosmic Intelligence will be quite undisturbed; It will let us go our own way without interference.

Humanity has reached a very high degree of development, that is obvious, and it owes this development to the powers of the intellect. Of itself the intellect is neutral, neither inherently good nor evil, but when the personality controls it — and this is usually the case — it becomes a very effective tool for the accomplishment of its most villainous schemes. Thanks to the extraordinary development of men's intellectual faculties, the personality is more and more successful in manifesting its most evil tendencies: the will to monopolize everything for itself and wipe out whoever and whatever stands in its way.

When I listen to some of the speeches by the leaders of political parties or trades unions, I can hardly help laughing. Whatever they do, it won't do any good. Why not? Because they themselves are not an example for anyone to follow, they are motivated simply by their own ambitions, their own prejudices; they are ruled by their personality. You will say that they are very intelligent people and very good speakers. Yes, I know; but that is not enough. They know all about politics, history and economics, but they are subjugated by their personality. When their individuality takes command, yes; then they will accomplish something useful. But do they even suspect that they have an individuality, a higher nature, and that it must be allowed to take control?

The present state of things will go on for years and years: there will be republics, democracies, wars, devastation and revolution. There are even some who are preparing for a third world war. But when human beings are almost at their last gasp, when they are so exhausted and worn out that they begin to long for a new order, then, perhaps, the great Masters and Initiates will come and assume the leadership and, in the presence of such splendour and justice, everyone will be ready to submit and obey. For mankind loves justice and order; if it has always been incapable of establishing a just, ordered society it is because, instead of choosing a ruler of a higher order, it has always chosen someone from the rank and file. If you choose your leader from

the common or garden ant population he will never be anything
but an ant. Human beings have never understood that they should
choose a being of another species. They always choose leaders
from their own ranks and those leaders are, of course, capable
of making speeches, arguing and biting, but nothing more, because
they know nothing about Initiatic Science. In fact, not only do
they know nothing about this Science, but they do everything possible to preserve and deepen their ignorance.

Everything could be magnificent and marvellous, but you have
to understand the reality of things. It is true that, in the past,
when there were kings, the population was the victim of much
injustice and cruelty and endured great tribulations. But is the
situation any better today? Can you prove that it is better? In
some cases, I admit, it certainly seems to be better. But behind
this apparent progress it is actually worse, for human beings don't
realize what they are missing. They are free to rub along in life,
to eat and drink and amuse themselves, but this freedom is not
really progress; it is still a form of servitude. Young people,
especially, want to be free but only in order to do all the wild
things that come into their heads. They fail to see that this makes
them the slaves of their baser inclinations and that they will be
obliged to keep feeding them. They are outwardly free, yes; but
they are inwardly bound. This is how human beings understand
freedom. But that is not enough; it is not enough to win external
freedom by means of war and revolution. It is inner freedom that
has to be won, freedom from one's own weaknesses, one's own
greed, one's own vices.

I have often compared this situation to that of a ship with
its captain and its stokers. The stokers, who work below decks,
are not in command; they are not able to see where the ship is
going or to keep it on course; they haven't been given the necessary
faculties. But they are fully able to keep the ship moving;
everything depends on them. In the same way, a country depends
on the masses for, if they were not there to do the work, everybody
would starve to death, including the aristocracy. But it is no good

expecting the common people to be clairvoyant and omniscient; that is impossible. Their job is to sow and reap; without them, the result would be famine. But without the aristocracy, without the captain at the helm, the result would also be disastrous. In creating men's bodies, Cosmic Intelligence has designed them in such a way that they are living examples of the pattern that should be followed in all social organization. As a matter of fact, human beings have succeeded in groping their way towards a pattern that bears some resemblance to this ideal, but it is still very far from perfect. There are always those who rule and those who are ruled but they are not always where they should be.

The element that is lacking is a true respect for the right order of things in man himself and in society. I don't combat my inner populace; on the contrary, I take good care of them and keep them clean and tidy. Yes, my people are well looked after but they know that there is an aristocracy above them and that they have to obey it. No revolutionary songs about chopping off the heads of aristocrats for them! Quite the contrary, they respect and obey them.

Actually, I am in favour neither of an aristocracy nor of a democracy, but of an order that exists throughout the universe and is reflected in our own bodies. Why didn't Cosmic Intelligence put our belly on our shoulders and our head between our legs? It put the head above and the belly below and now people want the belly to be on top and the head anywhere except in its rightful place. No, you must understand that a universal order exists which is not exactly the same as that which human beings would like to establish. The crime of human beings is to want their own order, their own system, their own point of view to take precedence over that of Cosmic Intelligence. Their personality is so avid to have the upper hand and impose its will that it is ready to topple the Lord Himself from His throne. It is man's personality that is the cause of all misfortunes; it has already led to the destruction of several civilizations.

The question is very serious, my dear brothers and sisters. You must study this question of the personality and the individuality[2].

The Bonfin, September 11, 1977

2 See *Complete Works*, vol. 11, 'The Key to the Problems of Existence', which studies this question in detail.

IV

The Book of Genesis tells us that one night, while Jacob was asleep with his head on a stone, he had a vision of a ladder pitched between earth and heaven, and going up and down the ladder was a host of Angels. This is how Jacob received the revelation of the celestial hierarchy that links earth to Heaven. The earth is linked to Heaven and an uninterrupted flow of exchange takes place between them which is rarely mentioned, even by Initiatic Science. For example, when Moses wrote, 'In the beginning God created the heavens and the earth', he did not mention any exchange or intercourse between them. One might conclude from this that heaven and earth were quite separate. In fact, this is what human beings have often thought: that heaven and earth were two distinct, even alien, realities. The truth is, on the contrary, that they are in constant communication; without this communication nothing would make sense.

Heaven and earth, or if you prefer, sun and earth. Between the two there is an ongoing exchange and it is this that produces life. At the moment, we cannot see very much of this exchange. All we see are the sun's rays that reach us, on earth; we see nothing of what rises from earth to the sun. Only clairvoyants are able to see the multitude of beings who descend from higher regions to do their work with the plants and stones of earth and who, once their work is done, rise again to the heavens. Actually, there is a quite a lot of extraordinarily beautiful and poetic literature on this subject and, one day, the whole of mankind will be capable of seeing these creatures who come and go between earth and the sun — and even more distant regions. When this day comes we shall enjoy perfumes and quintessences as yet unknown and hear the music that resounds throughout space, for everything in the universe sings. Everything in the universe is music.

But let's get back to this idea of hierarchy, for it is extremely useful for our inner life. If we know that everything — from the stones of the earth to God Himself — is linked hierarchically, and if we keep this structure constantly in mind, we are bound to act accordingly and do what is right, for we see that everything fits in to that order, that organization, that system. Hierarchy is a state of perfect harmony in which each element is in place. This applies in every domain and, if most human beings are so unhappy, it is because they do not respect this hierarchy. Their belly is where their head or their heart should be and vice versa. There is no order.

Suppose you go to a village and look for the school. Even if you don't know where it is, you won't need to ask your way: you can go straight towards the shouts and screams you hear coming from the children and there will be the school. But then, all of a sudden, the noise ceases and silence reigns. What has happened? The school master has arrived, that's all, and all the little ragamuffins that had been climbing on the desks and benches and making so much noise, are sitting in their places looking like little plaster saints. Isn't this a manifestation of hierarchy? Hierarchy means everything and everyone in his place. And, as I say, this is true in every domain: in our bodies (in which water must not get into the lungs, for instance, nor air into the stomach), in towns and cities, in government departments, in the army, in an orchestra, etc., etc.

Every human being has a place that is his by right. Unfortunately, this right is not respected in present-day society in which the worthiest and most intelligent people are unknown, whilst those who are violent, corrupt and unscrupulous are in command. Even in men's inner lives this hierarchy is rarely respected: the entities and forces that should be in command are absent and others have usurped their posts. I assure you, this is so. Look at anyone you like: who rules him? Do you imagine that he is king of his own realm? Not a bit of it; he is languishing in a prison cell where he receives barely enough bread and water to keep him alive, while others − dark, chaotic, unknown forces − rule in his stead. Naturally, he suffers from their tyranny and is constantly ill-treated, but he is obliged to obey them. Actually, he is not sufficiently conscious to understand that he is no longer the captain; although his ship is drifting out of control he believes that he is still at the helm.

Until man once again accepts this notion of a heavenly hierarchy, he will continue to drift towards anarchy. This is what is so serious: external anarchy does not matter so much, but inner anarchy is very serious. It is because of this inner anarchy that hospitals, mental homes and prisons are always full of patients and criminals.

Listen well to what I am saying: you can travel throughout the world, you can explore all the regions of space, you can enrol in all the schools of Heaven, and everywhere and always you will find this notion of hierarchy with God in command at the summit and all His creatures standing ready to carry out His commands. And, when you achieve this hierarchy in your own inner life, everything within you will sing. Your very cells will sing and you will feel yourself cradled, born up by an extraordinary state of harmony and music.

But this harmony will not be restored until everyone and everything is where they should be and, to achieve this, we have to begin at the beginning and put the heart and the intellect back where they belong. Most human beings are ruled by their emotions and passions; their intellect can do no more than say 'Amen'

and hasten to obey. But this is anarchy! And people don't even
know it; in fact, if you tell them that they are living in anarchy,
they take it as an insult. But I repeat: as long as the heart and
intellect are not in their respective places, it is the reign of anarchy. Have you ever wondered why Cosmic Intelligence placed our
heads above our hearts? As I have already told you, it is exactly
the situation of the ship in which the captain is up on the bridge
and the engines below decks. Our engines drive us forward but
it is the captain who decides what course to steer. Our engines
are our heart, our feelings; it is they that move the ship, but they
don't know what direction to take unless they are enlightened
by someone else, and that someone is the captain, our head, which
is on a higher level and can see where it is going. If you reverse
their positions and put the engines up on the bridge and the captain down in the bowels of the ship, that will be the end of it,
for the ordinary seamen have not been trained to do the captain's
work.

Everything is hierarchical. Even in the constellations of the
Zodiac: some stars correspond to the head of Aquarius and others
to the feet; in Aries, some correspond to the horns and some to
the hoofs. Or, take a river: from its source to its mouth a river
is hierarchical. Even in a tree, from its roots to its flowers,
everything is hierarchically organized.

You will ask, 'But how do we know where things belong? It
is a very complicated science.' Let me illustrate it for you: what
is the first thing you must do if you want to transform a desert
into a fertile plain? Find water. Bring in water and allow it to
flow, and everything else, plants, animals and men, will find their
place. The flowing water is the stream of life. Allow water to flow,
allow life and love to flow and don't worry about what kind of
trees will grow where or what birds will come and sing in their
branches. Some may say, 'Yes, but I want to know in advance
exactly where that clump of grass will grow and on which branch
the bird will perch to sing its song'. For goodness sake! If you
wait to find out all these details before making up your mind to

open the sluice gates, the centuries will go by and there will still be no flowers growing and no birds singing. Let the water flow, therefore; the water of life, the living water of love, and you will see how the hierarchical order begins to take root in you and everything slips into place; everything will start singing and blossoming and it will be the Kingdom of God.

From now on, therefore, work at this notion of the hierarchy that reaches all the way to the throne of God and try to see how you can achieve it within yourselves. You will have to pray and implore and struggle but, at last, the Spirit of God that you have been begging and praying for will begin to dwell in you and transform everything within you. When He comes, even if it is only for a second, everything will start to vibrate joyously, in harmony. But this cannot happen in the absence of your head. Without the head, there can be no hierarchy; only if the head is where it should be can it be achieved. It is possible for you to transform everything within you, all the impulses, currents and forces within you, but only by putting the head where it belongs, by putting the Lord at the summit of that hierarchy.

The idea of hierarchy is deeply rooted in human nature; even animals recognize it: they choose the strongest, most intelligent or most handsome of their number to be their leader and then obey him completely. Even animals know that worth must be recognized and respected. It is only human beings who have lost their sense of worth; they are too proud. Humility, you see, is a recognition of a hierarchical order. A person is humble when he recognizes superiority in another.

Of course, if I insist so much on this notion of hierarchy, it is because I always have in mind the inner hierarchy. A person can be at the top in external things and at the bottom inwardly. You can be at the top in society simply because you are rich or learned, but to be at the top in the eyes of the divine world you have to have something more than wealth and learning. In fact, it is easy to see this: you cannot make the spirits and forces that dwell in you obey you if you are not superior to them. They im-

mediately know exactly who and what you are and, if you are
no better than they are, nothing you can do will make them obey
you. Even if you try to give them orders in the name of Jesus,
they will scoff at you: 'We know who Jesus is, but who are you?'
In fact, not only will they refuse to obey you but they will give
you a good thrashing.

When one knows about this hierarchical order one is obliged
to work honestly instead of being full of recriminations. To be
angry and indignant about not getting what you want will get you
nowhere if you never work on yourself in order to earn it. The
hierarchy that exists in the spiritual domain will not be moved
by anger and revolt. In human society, you may be able to get
to the top by striking out at others and making a lot of commotion: you can see this in revolutions, wars and insurrections. But
that kind of behaviour won't get you anywhere with the spiritual
world; the only way is hard, persevering, tireless work. In this
way, yes; it is possible to rise to a level where you can command
your own inner forces as well as the forces of nature and, one
day, you can be a divinity. In the physical world, to be sure,
human beings push and shove and pull other people down in order
to take their place because they do not know the laws of hierarchy;
on this level there is neither humility nor hard work nor understanding, only violence and darkness but this is not conducive
to the evolution of those concerned.

This is a law: human beings may receive *only* what they deserve
and must receive *all* that they deserve. This is a universal law,
a law promulgated by the Twenty-Four Elders. The forces of
nature know exactly what you do, what you are capable of and
what you deserve and they organize things so that, sooner or later,
you receive exactly what you deserve. But most human beings
know nothing about this law; they don't believe in the existence
of just, clairvoyant beings of a higher intelligence who honour
the law, so they resort to evil, violent, treacherous means to get
what they want and, eventually, of course, the forces of nature
have to teach them a hard lesson. Initiates know this. That is why

they never waver from their path; they know that the difficulties and misfortunes they meet on the way are only temporary, that these difficulties are useful, sometimes even necessary and that, in the long run, they will be rewarded as they deserve.

No one can take the place of another. God has given every single creature a particular vibration and a particular place in the universe. On the physical plane, of course, someone who is unscrupulous and dishonest can eject a rival and take his place but, on the spiritual plane, that is impossible. The place that God gives to each one is exactly the place he deserves. In this respect, justice is always absolute; there can be no unfairness. No creature can ever take the place of another, therefore, but each one must grow and develop so as to reach the perfection that God has envisaged for him and, when he reaches the fulfilment intended by God, he will be unique and irreplaceable for all eternity. No other creature in the whole universe will be the same. Even if others are more important, each one is king in his own domain, because it was God who gave him that domain. Through his life, each creature secretes a particular quintessence which belongs to no one else. Other individuals may be greater but their quintessence is of another nature, so no one can replace or substitute for another. Every single creature is irreplaceable.

The best people often appear to be treated unjustly by life but, if they really are 'better' and if they are undeterred by their difficulties, Heaven and earth have sworn to give them their due. This has always been so for everyone, and it will always continue to be so. What have we got to worry about, then? There is no need to worry about whether these forces are intelligent or whether they have gone to sleep and forgotten about us. The only thing we need worry about is whether we are doing our work as we should, for these entities are perfectly capable of doing theirs and, when the time comes, they will give us the kingship that is our due.

Picture a young prince who, from his earliest years, has been entrusted to a family of peasants to be brought up in a simple, rigorous way of life. He doesn't know that he is heir to the throne and he goes to work every day dressed in rags and with just enough food to keep body and soul together. One day, after years of hard work, his apprenticeship is over and a procession of courtiers comes to fetch him away in a gorgeous coach. He can't understand what is happening; he thinks it is all a mistake; he doesn't realize that he had only been sent there so that he would learn to work hard, get up early and live soberly (Because, of course, you know how young princes behave if they are brought up in luxury: they grow up to be lazy, capricious and cruel!). When the prince gets to the palace and the courtiers want to know what he would like for lunch, he asks for some bread and cheese, an onion and some water. Naturally, they are in despair at this because the royal chef had already prepared a banquet of lobsters and turkey with the best wines. And suppose I were to tell you that you are all princes and princesses, sons and daughters of God, that God has entrusted you to a family of peasants — symbolically speaking — and that, one day, He will send an official delegation to fetch you. Yes, but on condition that you have worked well; otherwise your apprenticeship could last for centuries.

So there you are, there is nothing for it but to change the head and comply with that new head, and then everything else will change, too. We see this so often, even in everyday life. If a new President is elected, for instance, he immediately forms a new government with new ministers and a whole new administration. Why does he do this? Why doesn't he leave the same men in charge? Because he knows that it is impossible: the law of affinity, of magnetic attraction makes it necessary to inaugurate a new hierarchy, a new order. If the new leader is a gangster, he will give all the important posts to his own men, and a period of disorder and gangsterism will ensue. This is a universal rule: as soon as someone new takes command, he dismisses the old staff and gives their jobs to his own cronies, his own family and friends. How can you object that it is useless to change the head, that things will always be the same? Not at all, once the head is changed, everything else changes; every post is taken over by someone who is in agreement with the head. If the new head is a crook, therefore, all the other crooks will come out of hiding and give him their support and, if he is a saint, all the other saints will rally round him and fit into his administration as though they were old friends.

You can see, now, why the very best thing for a disciple to do, is to place the best and most magnificent Head of all — that great White Head whose beard and hair are described in detail in the Cabbalah — at the summit of his being. If a disciple succeeds in giving the Lord the very highest place within him, Angels and Archangels will also come and dwell in him to keep the Lord company. The Almighty cannot bear to be in the company of demons, so they are immediately dismissed and His Heavenly hosts come and sing round Him. It is impossible that it should be otherwise!

The only true transformation, the only true alchemy, the only true magic is this: to change one's head. And, in order to change his head, a disciple must, at the very least, be ready to say, 'I don't wish to be in command. I want to be a servant; I want to work and to obey. I want the Lord to come and dwell in me.' And then he must work as hard as he can for this to come about. In the end, when He sees that conditions are right, the Lord will come and, when He comes, all the spirits of light will come with Him and fill all the available space. You see how simple it is? You only have to change the head and all the rest changes, too; it cannot be otherwise. How could the Lord, once He had decided to dwell somewhere, find Himself all alone or in the company of demons? Unthinkable! Wherever He goes He is accompanied by a retinue of extraordinarily beautiful entities. If you take the trouble to understand the meaning and value of the hierarchy, you will be capable of fantastic realizations.

Vidélinata (Switzerland), March 25, 1962

V

I have already spoken to you, many years ago, about the underground kingdom of Agharta and the fantastic civilization that has flourished there for thousands of years. This hidden kingdom is in communication with the surface of the earth; there are openings in many different countries in the world: at the Poles, in South America, Mongolia and Tibet, and even in France, in the Pyrenees. From time immemorial, especially in the countries of the north, there have been legends that tell of a land beyond the icy wastes of the Pole in which it is always springtime. And, according to a tradition known to Initiatic Science, the aurora borealis is produced by very highly evolved beings who dwell in that kingdom with light from the centre of the earth.

There have been people who were aware of the existence of Agharta. There was even a film, *Lost Horizons*, which was about *Shangri-La*, the land of perpetual youth. In every country the tradition has existed and, whether in Greece, India, Egypt or elsewhere, this mysterious subterranean kingdom has given rise to belief in a land of eternal youth and happiness which has been known, sometimes, as Agharta and sometimes as the Land of the Holy Grail, Thule or the Garden of the Hesperides.

Today, more is being said and written about Agharta but, not so many years ago, it was virtually unknown. A Russian writer,

Ossendowski, published a book called *Beasts, Men and Gods* in which he recounts what he learned about Agharta in the monasteries of Tibet. But it was the Marquis Saint-Yves d'Alveydre who made the most striking revelations in his book, *The Mission of India in Europe*. Saint-Yves d'Alveydre was a writer, a scholar and an Initiate; he was capable of out-of-body travel and, in this book, he tells of how he visited and saw Agharta for himself. He gives many extraordinary details about this subterranean kingdom, about how it is lit by a kind of internal sun, about the trees and flowers growing there and about the animals and men who live there, just as on earth. He describes the libraries and archives which stretch for miles and which contain the whole history of the human race. Yes, there are some amazing books there, books written by great Initiates and containing great secrets. These books were taken away from human beings but they are still there, in Agharta, and only those who are sufficiently evolved have the right to go and read them.

Everything that has happened in the world since its beginning is recorded and preserved in these archives. All that has disappeared from the face of the earth and that we believe to be lost to us for ever, is there, in those archives. If you wonder what some historical figure was like, this is where you will find the answer. And you, too, are there, in miniature. For there is a copy of every one of us and it is kept there so that we can be studied. Every single thing that happens here is reflected in miniature in Agharta; in fact, at this very moment, the Aghartans know that I am talking about them.

Some people, who have done some research in this connection, think that the first Gypsies (or Romanies) were banished from Agharta and that it is from there that they draw their special knowledge of the Tarot, for example, which they hand on from generation to generation. It is also believed that the Aghartans first came from Atlantis and Lemuria. Before the continent began to submerge — some researchers put this at fifteen thousand years ago — they are said to have fled in their extraordinary machines and taken refuge in the bowels of the earth, where they built cities and settled down.

To be sure, there are all kinds of extravagant theories about Agharta, but I am not interested in knowing whether they are true or false. What does interest me is the underlying philosophy, the principles on which this kingdom is founded and how to propagate this philosophy amongst human beings. And what interests me above all is how to get human beings to understand that if they continue to follow their false philosophies, they will soon come to a bad end.

The kingdom of Agharta is organized and ruled with immense wisdom and its millions of inhabitants live in prosperity, peace and happiness, free from disease and old age. Saint-Yves d'Alveydre describes this organization in detail. At the top, he says, is a trinity of beings: the Brahâtma, the Mahâtma and the Mahanga (whom Ossendowski calls the Brahytma, the Mahytma and the Mahynga). Authority belongs to the Brahâtma, power belongs to the Mahâtma and the Mahanga is in charge of organization. And, as the government of Agharta is patterned on that of the universe, below this supreme trinity is a group of twelve persons that reflect the twelve signs of the Zodiac; under them is a group of twenty-two, reflecting the twenty-two principles of the Logos with which God created the world and, finally, there is a group of three hundred and sixty-five, reflecting the three hundred and sixty-five days of the year, etc.

I have reflected and meditated for years and years about Agharta and worked constantly to make contact with this invisible kingdom and, although you may not believe this, the time has come to tell you that I am bringing you the same pattern of organization that prevails there and which is known as synarchy. It is high time that human beings realized that they have never yet found the best type of government and that only a synarchy, a government of Initiates, can solve all their political, social and economic problems.

I am offering you the same culture as that which exists in

Agharta. I have never been in a position to reveal it fully because I know that if I divulged it, it would seem so remote, so unthinkable, that I would be in danger of being locked up. I assure you, if I were to say all that I know I would soon find myself in an asylum. This is why I dare not reveal certain things to you. But it is all here, in my head and, little by little, I am leading you into this world of Initiatic truths. In any case, if you are honest, you cannot help but admit that everything I have revealed to you so far has been true. I leave you free, therefore, to do as you wish.

But one thing is absolutely true, and that is that I am bringing you an entirely new culture. The Teaching of the Universal White Brotherhood has the mission to introduce the philosophy of Agharta into the world. There is a tradition that after Râma had established the Golden Age on earth, he went to live in Agharta. Many other great spirits such as Buddha, St John, even the famous alchemist, Nicholas Flamel, also went to Agharta when they left this world. But one thing that people don't know is that there are Aghartans who have reincarnated on earth in our day in order to bring us their science, their organization and their form of government: government by Initiates.

I can tell you about how the Aghartans live, how they are born and how they understand love. They know how precious sexual energy is, for instance, so, instead of squandering it, they use it to rise to greater heights of perfection and become divinities. As a matter of fact, the true doctrine of Tantra-yoga, which is so widely known in Tibet and India, comes from Agharta. Very few Westerners understand – still less practise – this form of yoga correctly. Many of those who have tried it, in fact, have only succeeded in making themselves ill and destroying their emotional balance. Be careful, therefore: I don't advise you to embark on experiences in this area. Study well, prepare yourselves, purify yourselves and, when you are ready, the extraordinary science that these beings possess will be revealed to you.

The science of the Aghartans also includes the most advanced

discoveries of physics. They are capable of seeing and controlling all that happens on earth. In fact, if they wanted to, they could
unleash the power of the four elements and wipe out the whole
of humanity. Fortunately, they are too peace-loving and much
too highly evolved to do so. It is also very likely that flying saucers,
whose existence is no longer in doubt, come not from other planets
but from the centre of the earth via the North or South Pole.
Many observers in the Arctic and Antarctic regions have seen flying saucers coming or going in the direction of the Poles.

In any case, the Aghartans have some extraordinary means
of transport and it is particularly interesting to note that it was
in 1945, after the atomic bomb that wiped out Hiroshima, that
they began to manifest themselves more frequently. They come
to keep an eye on us; they are concerned because they know that
human beings are quite capable, in their folly, of wiping out
humanity and, of course, if this happened it would also affect
them. It is possible that, within the next few years, they decide
to show themselves and give human beings some messages, some
warnings. And it is also quite possible that they will take some
of you back with them so that you can see the splendour of their
land for yourselves before coming back to earth. So far, none
of those who have visited Agharta have ever come back. But the
Aghartans are very, very kind and generous: you need have
absolutely no fear of them. They have overcome all human
weaknesses.

To be sure, quite a number of pilots have tried to pursue their
flying saucers but they are surrounded by a magnetic field that
makes them invulnerable: if they are pursued by a plane, they
can throw out rays that make its engines cut out. They always
work with light. Their source of power is light, and it is with this
that they neutralize all hostile forces. They apply the Initiatic rule
that it is light that must be our protection against harmful
elements. Before very long, human beings will begin to discover
many of their secrets.

I have been telling you this for years: the only thing you must study is light, for light is all-powerful. Science has recently discovered the power of the laser, but there are many more discoveries to be made. One day, all the revelations I have made to you will be recognized and published at large. So far, they have not been taken seriously because they have not been confirmed by orthodox science. Instead of sensing their authenticity inwardly, instead of touching them, as it were, with their soul and spirit, human beings are so over-intellectual that they prefer to wait for the verdict of science before believing even the greatest truths. But, I repeat: sooner or later, all that I reveal to you in my lectures will be scientifically proved. This is already beginning, in fact, with experiments that are being made in Russia; the other countries are behind Russia in this but they, too, will come to accept the reality of the aura, clairvoyance and the power of thought. Technicians have perfected instruments that can now measure some so-called 'para-psychic' phenomena and this means that people will be obliged to accept the results recorded by them. Human beings don't trust the instruments placed in them by the Creator: they ignore them completely, preferring to wait for the verdict of an external instrument, whereas it should be just the other way round.

As I have said, I am interested in Agharta from a philosophical point of view, because of the pattern of organization, government and collective life it presents. We, too, should work for the collectivity with the same disinterestedness and the same tireless love as the Aghartans so as to form a single family on earth, so that there shall be no more boundaries, no more war, no more poverty. When this is achieved, the interests of individuals will be protected. In a prosperous, healthy collectivity, each individual member also thrives, whereas, if only a handful of individuals prosper within a collectivity riddled by poverty and dissension, they will always be at risk, for their prosperity is not built on anything firm and lasting. This is why, when we see that every individual is interested only in his own well-being and cares nothing for that of others, we can be sure, in advance, that it is an unstable situation. If human beings would only make the effort to forget about themselves a little more and devote themselves to the good of the collectivity, the interests of every individual would be protected. For the good of the individual is in the good of the whole. This is why I keep telling you that you don't know where your own best interest lies; your behaviour proves this and, sooner or later, it will be your downfall.

The life of the collectivity surrounds, dominates and rules us. We can never be free and independent of it. This means that you must stop trying to find a comfortable little niche for yourself because it can never be anything more than a stop-gap. Unfortunately, human beings are still a long way from this expanded consciousness. They are like insects: as soon as something goes wrong they scuttle off into their little hiding places thinking that they will be safe there. Well, that is fine, it is something that we have inherited from the insects, but surely we are capable of changing just a little. To be sure, human beings have already made progress where the collectivity is concerned, but not enough: they continue to massacre each other. Their consciousness has expanded slightly, that is true, but the situation has not really changed much. In the past, one man would be killed where, today, millions are killed at one stroke. That is progress for you! Ah, yes; human beings have made great progress. They have built much bigger towns, for instance, but their inner nature is unchanged: each person remains isolated in his own little hole. They are still 'troglodytes' just as they have always been: isolated, divided and hostile.

The solutions men need must be sought on a higher level, in the spirit, in light. As long as they keep trying to solve their problems without that light, even the most far-reaching political and social transformations will never be truly effective for they will always contain the germ of a personal interest which runs contrary to the collective interest and which will end by contaminating all the rest. Men must consult that eternal wisdom that the

Aghartans consult and that I myself always consult, and it will show them what to do. As it is, even the Church doesn't consult this higher wisdom; it has substituted its own interests for the interests of the Lord. This is why the prophecies of Fatima are so terrible for the Church. But people no longer believe in anything; self-interest and money have priority over everything else.

I know very well that, because of this, the system that I bring you has no chance of being either understood or applied. In fact, if certain authorities realized that our Teaching was based on the synarchy, they would be quite capable of trying to close us down. They hate the synarchy! But conditions are going to change and, before long, no one will be able to stop these truths from spreading. No one! The Age of Aquarius is coming closer and bringing with it its Teaching of the collectivity.

The synarchic order will be established and will prove itself. Every system has to prove itself and, when it turns out to be ineffective, is replaced by another and then another, and so on. This is how men grope their way forward until, eventually, they find the right solutions. In reality, instead of continuing with an endless succession of painful and very costly experiments, it would be possible for men immediately to adopt a system that has been in existence for thousands of years. Unfortunately, at the moment, everyone wants to experiment and discover the great truths for himself. True, this is one way of doing it. Eventually, everyone will reach his goal this way, but it will take a very long time – hundreds if not thousands of years. The Creator has given all human beings the same ability to arrive at the truth, but the time that this takes is not the same for all. Those who accept to be instructed and guided by a Master save themselves a great deal of time, expense and suffering, whereas those who refuse this rapid and effective means will arrive at the same truths but thousands of years later. They prefer to tread a lone path; they want to be free and refuse to submit to or follow anyone else and, although they will eventually reach their goal, it will take them a very long time.

This attitude is particularly prevalent amongst intellectuals. Every now and then, one finds an exception to the general rule, but they are rare. I myself am one of those exceptions. Fortunately for me, Providence saved me by depriving me of all kinds of intellectual faculties that others have received in abundance. This is why I have been so ready to accept the wisdom of others who were more advanced, whereas those who have great intellectual gifts believe themselves to be capable of doing things by themselves. It seems to me that Providence has not been quite so kind to them: they refuse every authority and rely exclusively on their own resources, with the result that it will be thousands of years before they discover the truth.

In a few years from now some very important discoveries will be made. The only question is whether there will be enough human beings capable of understanding and feeling them and putting them into effect in their lives. It says in the Bible that everything will be revealed at the end of time. And this time is near. Of course, when it says 'the end of time', we must not imagine that it means the end of the world. The end of the world has already been announced time and again – even the date has been specified – and people have been struck with terror and prepared to die. And then the fateful day arrived and passed ...and the world went on as usual. Occasionally some minor upheaval occurred, but the world continued to go round. Mankind will never completely disappear. Human beings are tough, don't worry! They can survive anything. But there is no doubt that there will soon be all kinds of upheavals and changes and that it will be the end of an era. In his book, *Beasts, Men and Gods*, Ossendowski tells of how, one evening, he was with a caravan of camels, crossing a great plain in Mongolia when, all of a sudden, everything fell silent (Saint-Yves d'Alveydre mentions the same phenomenon): men and beasts stood still, even the birds did not fly. His guide explained that this awed silence fell over all things in nature whenever the King of the World entered the sanctuary in his subterranean palace in Agharta to pray. Very few human beings have ever seen the King of the World but, every now and then, he has appeared on the occasion of a religious holiday and his appearance is always accompanied by great prodigies. He has also made certain prophecies, some of which have already been realized and others of which are still to come. Yes, the King of the World does exist and he is waiting for the right moment to manifest himself. Also, as I have already told you, some beings from Agharta have incarnated in the world today in order to carry out the plans of the Invisible World. Many of them are working, even now, for a world government.

Try to understand what I am telling you: above is the New Jerusalem, the *Ierouschalaïm Hadascha* of which St John speaks, and below is Agharta whilst we, human beings, are between the two. When the New Jerusalem descends and Agharta rises from below, the Kingdom of God will be established amongst men. Agharta, like the New Jerusalem, denotes the inner life. It was to Agharta that the alchemists referred when they used the word VITRIOLUM, each letter of which is the initial letter of a word in the Latin sentence: '*Visita Interiora Terrae Rectificando Invenies Occultum Lapidem Veram Medicinam*', which means, 'Visit the bowels of the earth; rectifying you will find the hidden stone, the true medicine.' Agharta is also this inner earth into which we must penetrate[3], for man is made in the image of the universe and all that exists outside him exists, also, inside him.

Vidélinata (Switzerland), March 17, 1974

---

3 See *Complete Works*, vol. 6, chap. 10, 'The Hara Centre'.

By the same author :
(translated from the French)

Izvor Collection

PRINTED IN FRANCE IN JUNE 1990
EDITIONS PROSVETA, Z.I. DU CAPITOU
B.P.12 – 83601 FRÉJUS CEDEX
FRANCE

– N° d'impression: 1809 –
Dépôt légal: Juin 1990
Printed in France